What Others Are Saying about This Book …

"From time to time, people appear unto us so as to jolt us into consciousness. Life has gifted us with Patricia Gagic, and she handles this assignment with grace." **—Glenn Morshower, Actor (IMDb) and Motivational Speaker, "The Extra Mile Seminars"**

"In her exciting and soulful new book, Patricia Gagic shares how to gain expedient wisdom by leaving your excuses behind, and shows you how to MASTER the 'Five Radical Degrees of Life' so that you better live in a state of joyful, soulful, and purpose-filled abundance. Bottom line—this book ROCKS!" **—Craig Duswalt, Speaker, Author, Radio Host and the Creator of the RockStar System for Success—How to Achieve RockStar Status in Your Industry**

"Through her brilliance and her forward thinking nature, Patricia Gagic contributes a captivating perspective to the dialogue around wisdom and happiness. With a markedly inquisitive mind and many diverse experiences, she has gained an eye to the next generation as we seek to empower youth to embrace life to the fullest degree, we can all benefit from her wonderful insights." **—Craig Kielburger, Co-Founder of *Free the Children***

"Brilliant Patricia! Your book will help change many lives by helping alter many old mindsets so as to bring inevitable harmony within family, community and world." **—Nima McElhinney, Director, SuDiki Care Inc. (www.halseylodge.com)**

"This book is a true must-read if you are searching for your path." **—Dr. Budhendranauth Doobay, Order of Ontario, Chair-Canadian Museum of Hindu Civilization Leader of Vishnu Mandir Temple**

"Patricia Karen Gagic, is an inspiring example of a woman who uses her life to contribute to the world and make a difference in the lives of individuals. This book is a reflection of such positive and forward thinking." **—Amanda Owen, author of *The Power of Receiving: A Revolutionary Approach to Giving Yourself the Life You Want and Deserve* (www.AmandaOwen.com)**

"Patricia Karen Gagic is a wayshower—an elightened one who can lead humanity through spiritual and personal development. Read, listen and learn from *Karmic Alibi* ... and BE amazed." **—Kathy Doore, author of *Markawasi Peru's Inexplicable Stone Forest* (www.markawasi.com)**

"*Karmic Alibi* is a revelation and MUST READ—Patricia's experiences bring a depth of insight, empathy and an intuitive honesty that is changing the world...a Spiritual Spitfire!" **—Donna Kim Brand, International Teacher, Facilitator (www.DonnaKimBrand.com / www.GameChangerThinking.com)**

"Patricia Gagic came into my life during my darkest day; after losing my precious teen daughter to cancer. The previous three year battle and devastating loss had taken its toll, leaving me emotionally, physically and spiritually broken. Although many friends and colleagues were empathetic and wanted to help, no one knew what to do, or say, but Patricia did. She was able to support and hold my space for me as I healed. She has mentored me and it has changed my life. I am in complete awe of her knowledge/wisdom, her impeccable work ethic, her compassion, her endless energy, and most importantly her passion for helping others, and commitment to making the world a better place. She works tirelessly behind the scenes, a backroom warrior, allowing "us" to be the ones in the spotlight, reaping all the rewards. She takes such pride in others successes, it is truly humbling. I could go on and on... if I sound overly enthusiastic, it is only because you haven't experienced her magic yet, but you will soon know what I mean. You are in for a life changing experience. As you read this remarkable and insightful book, let Patricia hold your space as you grow into the life you could have only imagined." **—Sharon Babineau C.D., International Speaker, Workshop Facilitator, author of *The Girl Who Gave Her Wish Away* (www.Mindbreak.ca)**

“Congratulations on your launch of *Karmic Alibi*. It is a book that can fundamentally shift how we think and evolve during our precious time here on Earth. The focus on creativity can be applied in our personal and professional life.” **—Dianna Dinevski, MBA, Research Executive Assistant, Applied Research & Innovation, Sheridan College, Oakville, ON**

“Patricia and I have been dear friends for many years and I have seen her not only help transform my life for the better, but many, many others! Patricia is AN AMAZING SOUL with so much wisdom. It is a privilege to know her and call her one of my great mentors. I know this book will change lives and create more peaceful warriors in this world. Great Work!” **—Brian Melo, Recording Artist/Singer Songwriter, 2007 Canadian Idol Winner (www.brianmelo.com)**

“I have been in the business of speaking and training for many years and never have I seen anything like *Karmic Alibi*. I absolutely love the concept and the program designed by Patricia Gagic. I am positive that people will be captivated by her energy and wisdom and by this book their lives will be changed forever.” **—Judy Suke, President, Triangle Seminars, Motivational Humorist, College professor, Author (www.triangleseminars.com)**

“Do not hesitate in picking up *Karmic Alibi*. It is vital to the change you want to see in yourself, your business and your personal relationships. This book is so well rounded it will effectively permeate all aspects of your life. If you are honest with yourself as you read these pages, you will have no choice but to succeed.” **—Ruth Church, RMT (www.ruthchurchrmt.com)**

“I simply love the way you say these words with such clarity. Your words to paper are the Golden letters beaming poetically off the page.” **—Sheilagh Mercer, Life Is...Spirit Reflections in Art Animal Communicator**

(See more Testimonials in back section of book.)

Dear Kyra
I love you &
Thank you for
Being the
Angel in my
life!!
Karmically Connected
Yours in wisdom

KARMIC ALIBI

Gaining EXPEDIENT Wisdom by Leaving your Excuses Behind

Patricia Karen Gagic

Interior Layout Consultant: judysuke@bell.net

Interior Design: Jazmin Gomez

Bettie Youngs Book Publishers / Burres Books. Burres Books is an Imprint of Bettie Youngs Book Publishers. www.BettieYoungsBooks.com

If you are unable to order this book from your local bookseller, you may order it from *Baker-Taylor* or online from *Amazon* or *B&N*, or from *Espresso* or *Read How You Want*, or directly from the publisher, sales@BettieYoungsBooks.com

ISBN-Trade Paper: 978-1-940784-29-8

ISBN-eBook: 978-1-940784-30-4

Library of Congress Control Number: 2014944742

DEDICATION

This book is dedicated to Ned, for without these words, "From your mouth to God's ears" life would not be as it is, and to Kyra, Charlie, Cyris and Gabriel who ignited my heart with the spark of "Foreverness".

To my loving parents, Helen and my late father John Joseph; to the late Gary Byles and Jack Davidson with your pure love we have a story.

To Christopher, Sandra, Alexandra, Jeff, Rachel, and Julia, may you always know how loved you are.

All who have entered on the Path will know the equanimity by which this work serves. Those who dedicate their lives to the betterment of humanity I bow to you and embrace you with humility.

Contents

FOREWORD

Patricia Gagic's *KARMIC ALIBI* is written with a daringness and transparency I admire. Throughout the book she expresses the importance of trusting the voices within, and the natural unfolding of our lives. I seldom have the opportunity to dance with a kindred spirit, yet that is the prevailing sense every time I am in Patricia's midst. The ability to share aspects of one's life in a way that turns the event into a place where forgiveness, love and truth can be revealed is one of her genuine talents. Patricia has a heightened sense of awareness revealing sensitivity to humanity with directness yet a gentle understanding of the purpose of life. There is a state of gratitude revealed. Without doubt Patricia shares the power of the mind.

As a professional actor there are many times when "finding the character" within draws on life experience. Patricia shares with us multiple life changing events requiring a level of emotional management involving incredible strength and courage. I specifically felt the introduction of the Wisdom Auditor brought an awakening and illumination to expand our human consciousness. In this almost esoteric and mystical real journey there was a delicate rawness keeping me drawn in and captivated. From chapter to chapter she reveals an aspect of deep contemplation and raises the bar on the reader. In her unique style of writing there were complex layers of a genuine "soulness" that tied together throughout the book. I discovered another perspective within myself as I discern how life offers these challenges at times. Expect the unexpected in this revelation of truth and celebration of life. *KARMIC ALIBI* is filled to the brim with her compassion and intelligent, transformative thinking.

My description of humankind is that we are magnificent creatures behaving as if we're not. I refuse to see the world as pitiful. We are not unworthy. We are not disconnected.

We are spectacular creatures linked to the Divine, who experience that power to the extend we allow ourselves to. This is the very essence of what Patricia so effortlessly shares with us in *KARMIC ALIBI*. The world needs people to appear from time to time to jolt us into consciousness. Life has gifted us with Patricia Gagic, and she handles this assignment with grace.

—Glenn Morshower, Actor and Motivational Speaker, "The Extra Mile Seminars" (www.glennmorshower.com)

(Patricia Karen Gagic and Glenn Morshower in Los Angeles attending Craig Duswalt's RockStar Marketing BootCamp)

A WORD FROM THE AUTHOR

What are you doing with your precious gift of life? Human beings are part of the most spectacular, rare and Divine self-correcting consciousness. You happen to be one of them! Just for a moment let's pretend time does not exist and we are magically bound to this cosmic plethora of space and reality that offers us purpose, potential happiness and peace . . . in one lifetime. Such being the case, why would we choose a life unfulfilled? Do these choices we make in the illusory mind dictate our highest outcomes and best opinions? We often make choices based on our being victorious without consideration for the impact on others.

What if we could attune ourselves to consider mindfulness and enjoy the harmony and resonance of a stress-free life? We live in a world that begs us to respect and honor all sentient beings and treat one another with kindness and compassion, yet for so many these are words without meaning or action. Karmic Alibi is a story told in part as a memoir combining a spectacular revelation of transformational quality. Throughout the book there is tragedy, suffering, and joy. As I have found, one of the greatest lessons is to believe in your intuition and allow common sense to prevail. When you embrace *KARMIC ALIBI* you may feel the discomfort of a raw truth being exposed, and my hope is the voice inside your head will beg for you to stay there.

My desire is for you to find my experiences a healing tool for yourself. Think of it as a life maintenance tune up. The vision is to raise the bar on yourself and learn to access the root cause and begin cultivating new aspects of your true self, sitting dormant, waiting for you to show up!

If my story can reveal and activate the wisdom inside of you to locate a better way of coping, functioning and co-existing with more clarity and peace, the book will have served. Do you seek joy and satisfaction in your day to day lives? Do you desire to be of benefit to this world and become a very good world citizen? Karmic Alibi demands a renovation of our attitudes based on history, showing us it is absolutely imperative that we act "NOW". This might seem a daunting task, but once you make a personal agreement with yourself there will be an immediate realization you are shaving years off your potential suffering by projecting your future filled with all the great rewards of existence. Flirt all you want with the mirror of life, it will only serve you when you greet humility at the door, embrace the insights of your own wisdom, and recognize your true nature with self-love and compassion.

Walk into the spiral vortex of your own story with integrity and an inner knowing of how to redesign your future based on a greater understanding of this new-found awareness. From rags to riches of the heart you will begin to understand self-cherishing is the taskmaster wearing us down and tiring us out and at the end of our life has held us back from living with joy and contentment. When you learn how to appreciate your life, cherish every breath and serve humanity you will be empowered to realize your dreams. You can revive and rewire your future simply by giving up all attachment to what you thought was causing you to suffer. Imagine each member of the human race being able to manifest the highest and most precious outcomes for themselves and each other.

Through realizations, contemplations, visualizations, and meditations it is possible.

This is the best part of life, realizing you are one of the most important reasons for its existence.

You are a vital part of the stream of universal cosmic consciousness actively participating in its evolvement. You do make a difference to everyone and everything in this world. The world cannot live without you NOW.

"What are you doing with your Precious Gift of Life?"

The answer should be you are living in peace and equanimity. You are at the helm. What a shame it would be, knowing you have full control of your life and yet find an ALIBI that stops you short from discovering the elegant journey to full potential.

In the long run, we are all connected to one another and no matter how uncomfortable it can be these are the life lessons we have agreed to experience, and choices changing and shifting all aspects of our lives.

There are times when things converge and we find resolution. There are also times when we are face-to-face with our little dramas. Is it really necessary to stay stuck in the pain and suffering? In the emptiness of the mind there is the ability to be free. One day, we will lose one another in physical death leaving the past unrecoverable. Today can make a difference; why not make this effort and start NOW? Stop searching for an alibi.

As you read these recollections of my life they may cause you to wiggle and squirm a bit in your chair. If this happens, you are probably ready to enhance your tomorrows. Reflect upon your own experiences to find your karmic alibi.

Visualize and indulge in an authentic consideration; a willingness to examine your own life by taking off the rose-colored glasses. You may even open your heart and release attachment to your perception of suffering. The energy we manifest towards goodwill for all humanity is in our best interest. We are impermanent beings who selfishly ignore the damage we create by punishing ourselves and others refusing to see the impact it has on both this moment and the future. Dreams are reality, and excuses limit wisdom. Master the radical degrees of life.

◆◆◆

"Without a rich heart,
wealth is an ugly beggar."

—Ralph Waldo Emerson

PROLOGUE

Once upon a time when love was all that mattered and a second chance was begged for, the tadpoles found the Princess.

Often during conversations with my mother a sharing would take place. A flood of visions would be revealed to her and after long pauses she would awkwardly smile. Being able to describe my own birth has always baffled both of us. A conversation took place prior to the expulsion through the birthing canal and has repeated itself in both real and dream time. These visions are real.

Without hesitation, there was intense begging on my part to be human again. How does one know they had a prior existence? The need to be part of the continuum was granted, whether it was selfish or a Kwan Yin realization. Knowing so many suffer and having such a strong belief that every breath counts, the words became a mitigated discovery. There before me was a validation. The only punishment worse than hell, would be to leave this world without being on a path. One life is no more precious than the alchemical tricks we devote years chasing. Leave your mark in this world by serving, loving yourself and never forget each person you meet deserves your full attention. They are your karma.

The desire to find a petal in the mud is the path to creation and imagination driving the engine. Never stop looking or asking questions. The voices can be heard until emptiness arrives.

In 2009, while working in my art studio on two separate bodies of work, titled *"Avatar Within and Beyond"* and *"Illumination Within,"* there was an endless desire to write about my life instead of trying to paint it.

For over five decades the teachings of Christianity, Hinduism, Kabala, Buddhism and many others were constantly pursued. The Dharma and Catechisms revealed similarities and added more questions.

Reflecting on the value of one human life, it was obvious the ego was fuelled yet never satiated. A very dear friend commented one day on how my experiences had given her hope in overcoming her difficulties. She informed me of how my words had become emotional pain relievers and she encouraged me to formally teach others how to find inner solemnity and peace. Sometimes we hurt others along the way, always believing it was in everyone's best interest. After years of seeking, a tsunami of events formed the groundwork for this book allowing me to reflect and share the outcomes. Joy cannot be found when we hide behind manipulation and greed. The evidence reveals itself in confusion, abuse and denial, more commonly known as "excuses".

We have free will and make choices creating our mental, emotional and physical environments. There is much to gain if we learn to tap into our lives and unravel the pain associated with suffering. We are a plethora of wisdom and should never consider our lives to be less important or wasted.

In 2009 a phone call led me to meet Jigme Norbu the nephew of His Holiness the 14th Dalai Lama of Tibet on a highway near London, Ontario.

Jigme was following the tradition of his late father, Thubten (Takster Rinpoche) Norbu, by Walking for Peace.

He had endured over six thousand miles during twenty walks around the world. It became his mission to stand up for human rights and dignity. Jigme had decided to walk from Indianapolis to Toronto, an estimated eight hundred miles. Meeting him seemed like a moment frozen in time.

What transpired circled into a greater understanding of the Dharma and energized with urgency to act without judgment and stay aligned. It was a spiritual 'cloaking" that ripped the façade apart exposing the root of my suffering. Jigme undertook his need to serve with humility and penance. Whatever had transpired in his life motivated him to become a living warrior. He shared the importance to dedicate his life to World peace and asked us to make this same consideration.

On February 14, 2011 Jigme Norbu began the Peace Walk organized by the Ambassadors for World Peace. A three-hundred-mile walk scheduled to begin from St. Augustine, Florida to West Palm Beach. At 1:13 a.m. an email popped into my inbox from Jigme written before he was going to rest.

"Dear Patricia.... our karmic relationship is too strong for any obstacles to break it and as a matter of fact the purpose of this is our global campaign for World Peace".

The words were heartfelt and pure. What transpired at the end of day one of the walk changed the lives of so many. At 7:37 p.m. Jigme was accidently struck by a car and killed.

The shock of losing this warrior at the age of forty-five proved how delicate the balance is between birth and death.

His death challenged us to begin seeking the path towards the cessation of suffering. He believed it was achievable.

As you will learn in this book, it is our karma and for this there is gratitude.

Many suffer and struggle with their own demons, and cannot find peace within. The impetus to expose ones suffering and healing is regarded as transformational. The list of my mistakes is well known to me and the checklist of recovery always present. Whatever makes one act, respond to and dive in comes from a willingness to own it in the moment. It is compelling to see the outcome of these choices, days, months and years later. If you choose to be a judge of another, you reveal your own motivation. My belief is we not only act out of fear, but with carelessness. It is tough for some people to get up in the morning and face their little dramas, especially when others bring their interference. Greed is an evil sorceress and hatred is just confusion wrapped in ego.

We can live in a harmonious state on our beautiful planet Mother Earth if we learn to forgive ourselves knowing that no other person walks in our shoes. It is our job to love and remember our "Foreverness".

My decision to share these delicate scenes came from a deep examination of emptiness and impermanence. My path was woven with integrated love and pain from one source. Fortunately, well after more than fifty percent of my life has been lived, a transformation took place and there can be no regrets.

Mastering the *5 Radical Degrees of Life* were designed to offer a simple and inspirational tool towards gaining expedient wisdom.

Learn the steps via the FIVE RADICAL DEGREES: Risk, Root, Remedy, Realization and Reality. You will be enabled to reframe your life creating empathy, and overcome adversity by turning your karma into compassion and leaving your excuses behind.

"For every problem there is a solution.
For every question there is an answer.
For every action there is a reaction.
For every cause there is an effect.
For every thought there is an impact....
Everything is possible."

—Prince Randy K. Koussou Alam-Sogan Founder of Child of the Universe Project,Chairman of the African Global Alliance

◆◆◆

"Every time you are tempted to react in the same old way, ask if you want to be a prisoner of the past or a pioneer of the future."

—Deepak Chopra

One

THE PROMISE KEPT

"Dear God, please save the world! I promise to be a good girl and will dedicate my entire life to helping others if you save the world! I love you."

In 1962, the world was faced with the potential of War again. It was a time when a young, authentic Catholic girl believed that the world existed to "love". Six months before her tenth birthday she leaned hard on taking responsibility for herself and the world.

During the sixties home construction in some Canadian cities often included the building of a "bomb shelter" in the basement. Our home was one of those. A six-foot by six-foot room made of poured cement walls. The door was always locked. Curiosity permeated as the logic of living in a home filled with hugs and kisses also hosted a room without food, without water with an invitation for survival during times of crisis. There was a fear instilled inside me that year. The nightmare of living in a world equally as loving influenced my heartfelt desire to shed the suffering for those who somehow knew not how to pray for one another. It was an odd mindset to have yet one that somehow felt right.

In Grade five my imagination was stretched with a new kind of listening. Tapping on the door of impermanence in my tenth year of existence was the Opening of the Wedge to the Graduated path. There was an awakening one mystical day in April. All known to me was now being threatened.

How could the minds of so many people on this planet be driven to create such possible damage and chaos? During the first decade of my life there was protection from evil although it was shown to me each Sunday morning.

Now, the truth of human attitude was being revealed and it shocked me to my core. What motivated people to proclaim power over one another and believe that destruction of the earth and human lives was the answer? Tempered with tears and the feeling of aloneness all that previously existed was shattered inside my mind.

There was a corruption that could not be explained or examined. It wasn't rocket science to feel the hatred inside the words that were spoken each hour on the television. What was being birthed inside the hearts of our leaders? Nothing made sense to me. All of the adults who had entered my life were normal, loving, caring, decent and protective. Listening to the news that evening scared the living hell out of me. That was the first moment the realization of what power looked like became a reality. Not having the maturity of an adult it seemed ludicrous to accept what was happening. This blind induced corruption of mind control would not be accepted. My world was pure and unable to fathom the horror. This clearly wasn't my destiny and the moment to do something had arrived.

Quietly slipping downstairs to the basement while the rest of the family was glued to the television, my mission began.

Finding the keys hidden above the door frame gave me access to the bomb shelter soon to become my prayer room. The lights were left off and a flashlight became the moonbeam to guide me.

It took a few minutes for my eyes to readjust and become familiar with the interior of the prayer room.

It was the first time in my entire life that every cell in my body responded. My intentions were absolutely clear and precise. There would be an "ask, a promise and a result." Visiting the dark and ominous room made me feel very fragile and instantly vulnerable. The only time my feet had been inside this room was out of curiosity and lasted for less than three or four seconds. Very quickly my thoughts regrouped and the intentions were made priority.

Dragging a blanket from the playroom my father had built for us, a pillow was formed. My knees lowered and my head followed. Without hesitation my conversation began.

Dear God, my parents told me that you loved me. My parents love me. Father Breen at the Church tells me every Saturday morning at Catechism that you love your children. Why have you allowed some of your children to be evil? Doesn't everyone want to aspire to be an angel? Is being born in a human body punishment? The questions were relentless and eventually my thoughts diminished. Praying for the world to be saved from a nuclear war was all that my mind cared about. Begging for intervention and believing it would happen affirmed all things are possible with prayer.

My heart ached to the point of desperation that night. Praying incessantly believing that it was my job to save the world from destruction, my knees shook. Whatever took place between the cement walls and my conversation with God changed my future. There was no room for ignorance. All moments thereafter were reflections of my commitment to serve humanity. That is what happened. A pact with God was sealed.

At the age of nine, the experience of unbearable suffering took place. The suffering of the entire world fell upon me. There was peace of mind knowing people caught in their delusion and greed might be saved. Perhaps they would change. My belief included a cleansing of the mind as my prayers permeated the Universe through God. Whatever took place that night inked the way of my future.

One of the first questions that surfaced for me was how could so many people desire to co-operate with these conditions? Why would one wish to suffer and hurt others? It made absolutely no sense and there was no rational answer. Suffering was not an option. How could people feel joy, happiness and love while living with conditions of suffering?

Why were they so self-cherishing and filled with an indignant attitudes?

There was no logical explanation for me. My world only existed to love my family, my grandparents, neighbors, my cat Frisky and Mr. Smith my teacher! When my mind calmed and my final prayer was recited, "Dear God, please save the world" faith arose. It was done. The world was going to survive.

When morning came there was no bombing, the world was whole and going to school was happening. God had heard my prayers. God had answered my call. The telephone to heaven had been answered and the whispers were listened to. What transpired inside of me that morning became the evidence of faith. My voice took charge and responsibility for saving the world. That is exactly what my heart believed. God saved the world because of my prayers!

The corruption had dissolved. It was now my secret to live with "Forever-ness."

My gratefulness was obsessive. How could one ever repay the Omnipotent God when a favor was asked for and received? It was almost a curse. Each day my knees would hit the ground and prayers would begin, wondering if those who were corrupt and insane had rested their evil minds. Whenever news of horrific events were heard my hands quickly covered my ears and as my one "get out of jail" card had already been gifted.

The freedom eventually came when the spirit of generosity, perseverance and patience lifted me to realization.

There was a shadow that danced across the floor of the basement Prayer Room. My angel made himself known to me that night. Walking up the stairs after changing the face of the earth the Wisdom Auditor stood silently with me. At that very moment life became precious.

Two

KARMIC SCISSORS

Each morning before my feet hit the floor, my mind clears quickly, softly whispering," Thank you", because once again there is a morning being made available to me. Every day is a miracle. Why is that so? Why take for granted it will always arrive? Well, one day whether it was in a lucid dream state or my wires were crossed in my own reality the *Wisdom Auditor* showed up.

After spending years grappling with the mystery of who we are, what is consciousness and the purpose of life, a cosmic messenger arrived.

He spoke to me, *"Sweet girl, do you know each moment you have lived, each breath shared with humanity is all you have been required to experience? You have been on a sacred path to simply know the true nature of yourself and once the karma ripens you will no longer remain in the body you have come to know. These are facts one must ponder as the words remind us death is an obvious fact of life and inescapable."*

With razor sharp accuracy my eyes stared deeply into the face of the Wisdom Auditor and these words were whispered, "You need to enlighten me."

In the vacuum of this moment the quietude entered and the ordinary miracle of being alive today became the light of my shadow and the framework around all future moments. Those "little dramas" were immediately dissected in a potion comparable to formaldehyde. It was a revelation of their essence and life breathed into multiple realities.

Somewhere in the DNA of my being is a bar code with an expiry date hidden from my knowing, but it clearly does exist. There is no argument my fear of mortality was evident and best hidden away for another day.

Wisdom Auditor agreed and called me out, sharing by secretly creating ongoing reasons to stay in those dramas, layers of unhappiness and stress would thrive by virtue of my own conscious choices. My attachment to staying connected emotionally to everyone in my perceptions prevented my mind from being free.

The more attention given to all the chaos kept me sifting in between those layers not recognizing the impact and effect on both my physical and mental wellness. Here lies the conversation we should all contemplate with ourselves.

After many years of participating in the dance of life, the answer was being served up on a silver platter. Yes, all the curve balls finally straightened out and the humble truth was raw and naked. *"You have a choice and it has been carefully presented to you in each and every circumstance and relationship in your life."*

The Wisdom Auditor had cornered me, and it felt quite uncomfortable; like a harness being tightened around my chest threatening my very existence. Knowing this was part of the transformation my head tilted to the side and the re-runs began. Over and over there was a projection of images. These were life scenes never expected to be reviewed or repeated again. The examination caught me off guard and a great sadness entered, revealing how self-serving my motivations had been. There was immense pain in the ripples of confusion as there were countless others who were victims of my decisions. This weighed heavily on me, and running away was not an option.

Wisdom Auditor stood in front of me with golden scissors and smiled. *"Take these from me, close your eyes and search deeply to find the space where all time shines brightly and then simply let it all go. Allow the golden scissors to melt in the alchemy of all sensations and mysteries of life."*

"Patricia, you stepped out of safe and predictable and have risked an outcome. Now the hand of fate will reveal your destiny and karma."

"Would you agree by being free to observe with greater awareness, lis-

tening to your accurate intuition you might have prevented the pain and suffering you have endured? When we remove disease from our body we fully expect it will not return. Why not believe the mind is also capable of such an etheric surgical healing. Why not let go of holding weighted thoughts never able to lift a bridge? Take these karmic scissors and forever release yourself from suffering. Realize by purifying your mind you are also changing the karma of all those involved in your little dramas. Begin to feel the joy and embrace the happiness within as you disengage thoughts holding you prisoner."

Wisdom Auditor pressed into me and without any hesitation the idea became more desirable and soon the words were imprinted in my heart. *"This is the only moment to notice, pause and examine without judgment."*

There was an immediate sense of triumph and a humble redemption within. Are we not engineered as complex and unique creations of the Divine Sacred? Is the basis of all creation found in sameness? If we recalled all the chattering voices within our mind we would be dumbfounded at the struggle we bare.

We feed our belief we need to stand alone. The impetus to defend our fixation on what we think is the 'root' cause of all our suffering and depressions comes from within our own sense of survival.

The root of this examination comes to us when we decide our path is the priority of our individual purpose for living. The realms of existence beyond our comprehension will be there to experience after we balance our life as humans residing in this dimension on this glorious planet.

Our hearts and minds are one and the same. It is the gentle nature within guiding us to flourish in our spirit and soul. The voice reaches deep inside our minds knowing the difference. Why then can we not stand in our realizations and flourish bringing compassion and empathy to all our actions? The mirror never lies. The grasping into the spirit of our self-love is vital to survival. Do we ever really understand how the agents of greed and anger pry our hearts away from love? With knowledge comes the purity of wisdom and thus should eliminate the need to camp out on the doorstep of old narcissistic patterns.

We live in the most interesting of times. Sadness and suffering lurk around every corner seen both in the physical and mental, hand in hand with poverty and cruelty. There is an internal radar system available to each of us if we choose to tap in and listen to the revelations it exposes. Why do we eliminate equanimity from being part of our daily existence? How sad we think ourselves to be superior to one another, when we are all living out our karma. Whether this is living inside the dream or in between the moments, all our decisions count.

My hands formed a mudra and reached toward the Golden Scissors grasping them tightly. Wisdom Auditor smiled and the walk began.

The landscape and scenery were no longer identifiable. Ether filled the space with waves of soundless motion and gentle breezes. This simple eternity culminated into a dream-state and revealed itself in the mindscape with a feeling of pure emptiness. Barely able to focus, we appeared to be standing at the edge of a beautiful river. The paysage generated nirvana and eight massive mountains covered in blue snow dazzled with pureness and without shadow. The journey had just started yet very efficiently it felt as though the end was near. Describing details became overwhelming, as the clouds took on formless forms ship shaping and causing me to wince and skry looking for real angels to appear. Suddenly with the force of what felt like a million electrical volts my body fell to the ground.

There was an absence of love and hate.

The seconds turned into minutes and the minutes turned into the absence of time. This is my story NOW.

Three

INTERVAL BETWEEN THE WORDS

"Patricia, take a look," Wisdom Auditor beckoned me to join him. Slowly my body moved closer to him sitting at the edge of the bed. *"Dearest one, how have you found the strength to arrive here today?"*

With my heart pounding, my lips began to quiver and ever so carefully my head gently rested on his chest. The room began to spin and the luxury of being sober was gone as the subtle shift took me back to the place where Tiger Blood spilled.

Heady with the scent of musk my limbs felt the crushing of his body and the slamming into my tiny frame. With nothing to hold on to the room turned inside out and the black hole continued to dance like a whirling dervish out of control. The walk through the hall could have been described as the same walk a victim of genocide might have experienced. With the knowledge there was no escape route or evidence it would be successful by making a mad dash. This was not in the cards. Fear of being shot in the back was the outcome and it could not have come quicker. Resolved to fight, clenching through his lily white snake skin my finger nails ripped and bled from the wild thrashing. The ceiling became a kaleidoscope with hope written in rainbow colors. My eyes innocently smiled as my legs were held down and the blunt instrument was perfectly executed into my writhing body. The masterfully crafted spider web hidden in the corner of the ceiling in this insanity room offered me an invitation to escape. Desperately wishing there was someone home in this perfect web who would immediately drop down and pay a visit with a venomous sting. Unfortunately for me, no one was home. This was the Alice in Wonderland party where you were invited to not attend. This was the party no one was invited to, except me.

Had the guests forgotten what time they were to arrive?

I began to feel as if my performance was without a curtain call and never properly rehearsed.

What a shame my lack of experience was neither obvious to the neighbors or to the band loudly playing on the record player. If the word "evil" had not been invented before this particular night, it was then. In the distance my eyes caught the shadow and with remarkable timing, he managed to arrive. Silently and without disturbing the rattling of the floor; as the bed was now relocating across the room, the shadow captured my full attention. The quiet undisturbed yet familiar look in his eyes immediately, calmed me and my body began to relax and suspend into another dimension.

This was not an engagement of purity and there was no moment of ecstasy. At this point in my life there was no frame of reference to call upon and no way to know what should be happening. All my mind understood confirmed this was violent, wrong and eventually would rip my faith in trust into shreds. The painful twisting of fingers around my neck seemed to loosen and my voice no longer shrilled, it began to shrink. In the moments that followed the scent of delicate Forget-me-nots cruised around my nostrils and with a sigh of relief the sweat drenching the sheets began to cool. The bed was now free of the snake and the air was permeated with a fresh aroma.

Wisdom Auditor silently remained in the room.

It was an innocent invitation by someone of trust who now added their own spin on what fear should look like in my life. He had not been given permission, yet had taken control.

Even rabbits and snakes determine with elegance how they choose to mate. There is no name for the madness in an animal filled with a lust only saturated and quenched by the topical mercurochrome known as Tiger Blood. There was no trial inside these thin cement walls. Trust never even entered the court room of my mind. The hidden lawyers who stood side-by-side grinned as they remembered using the monkey and Tiger Blood themselves. There was an uncommon yet pathological intelligence only obvious to a victim. It seemed there was an unspoken bond or rite of passage between them. Given so little time for a defense the verdict remained and the outcome was a karmic alibi. Had my body agreed to arrive and walk down that hallway to the insanity room? Did my mind consent to the angry snake man who poured his Tiger Blood all over me? Would there ever be a time his motivation would be revealed sufficient for me to believe it was not personal?

Wisdom Auditor bent over my frail body and ever so gently helped me pick up the ripped and torn clothing strewn across the floor and no longer hugging my frame. The floor now had carved bruises and dents that would remain etched there forever. One could never walk across that floor again without the grave possibility a sliver might pierce the foot of the next victim. There was a sense of security, knowing perhaps my sacrifice had satiated the evil within this animal who called himself a man. His future desires had been quenched by the virgin he had captured. The last thought entering my mind was maybe he too had been a virgin and without doubt a coward.

When the mixture of my blood and sweat finally reduced and the mirror in the bathroom was no longer distant and foggy; my golden eyes caressed the shadow mysteriously playing hide and seek with me.

Wisdom Auditor held a firm and locked glance as my hands danced across my face cleansing this dirty memory.

What shocked me was finding myself to be completely alone in a house filled with secrets and one of them now mine. My body had become the battle ground and would always have a point of reference on the street without a name and number and now a notation in the Akashic records. The battle should never have been fought here, and in many ways my hope was this is where it would end.

Suffering attends to details. This was not my first, and unfortunately, not the last introduction to this sorcerer called suffering. The following hours seemed endless as my mind raced in between the words, in between the thoughts, and there was no calming the Tiger Blood. The walk home was frightening and all eyes including those in the back of my head were diluted with a toxic fear. Not running, walking or crawling could have made the journey less traumatic.

The ceiling in my bedroom had no spider web, no music or evidence of a recollection of madness.

To imagine facing those evil eyes again created a panic lasting an entire year. Our seats in school were only a few rows apart from one another. We were face-to-face every single day. His was no longer a face understood or trusted.

When the academic year ended my hidden eyes no longer felt the predator staring at me from across the room. The face of humanity had changed for me.

I had been raped of more than my innocence.

Eventually the fear associated with that night became an anchor and excuse for things not right. It became my karmic alibi. The taste of fear was always on my lips. The endless agony gripped every part of my existence. There was no relief from this stalker. Nightmares haunted me and the secret could not be buried no matter how many places my mind would seek out. This fear simply existed.

Anytime a story or news article would reveal the angst of someone who had been a victim, my heart wretched and ached with them. My prayers would be lined up like salt shakers on a window sill, praying they would recover and let the universe hold court. Never underestimate the power of karma.

Peace was welcomed when Wisdom Auditor sat at the end of my bed and let me find stillness within. There was no need to speak; he simply knew my thoughts. What does one think when all control is taken away? What does one do when the masked bandit without concern takes refuge inside of you?

The deep loss of this man's soul many generations ago prepared him well for this battle.

Had he chosen his Warrior Princess with keen and mindless effort or did he know? What is his karmic alibi? With deep concern about the future the question loomed "Is there ever a point when it makes sense?" How does one find forgiveness?

"My precious one, eventually the vibration of all who suffer will seek purity and cleansing. Perhaps, even now you have forgiven him without trial or punishment and have released the hatred existing in the dark shadow of your journey together."

"Consider opening your heart and sanction the army within him to become quiet. Imagine as his feet touched the slivered floor he felt the difference between a cactus and velvet. There will be a time when he will come face to face with his own warrior and demon. You have shown courage and a discipline inside your mind to detach from the physical moment of abuse. As traumatic as this was, he will suffer equally. You are not his jury. The teaching is in the angry realm of human existence. To torture a physical being in lust is the evidence of weakness and a shallow mind."

Thank you, Wisdom Auditor for finding me and holding me during the hours and days of my life. Is there nemesis?

"*Yes,*" replied Wisdom Auditor looking above causing me to sense another realm beckoned him. We walked down a hospital corridor together and came upon a window thick with condensation seeping between the layers making it difficult to see in. My eyes strained as they focused on a body ravaged with disease, his eyes hollow from immense suffering. Tiger Blood seeped from the pad on the stretcher.

We are impermanent beings. Love flourished within me and forgiveness permeated the filter between the past and present creating resolve. My hands touched the window hoping the sliver in his foot would feel less painful in his next life. His suffering was no longer mine.

"Death is not exclusive and your heart must continue to beat knowing this was a performance without an intended audience. You no longer need to feel shame or indulge in self-limiting experiences. The forgiveness you will generate must exceed and diminish your suffering in order to endure the underworlds of the future."

For all those who have lived through a traumatic experience it is very difficult to bring trust back into your life. What is in the physical is known to the mental and vice versa. What makes the art of life so perfect is the anonymity by which it arrives and leaves.

The Wisdom Auditor held my arms and with great determination walked me back through another door. This time, there was a sense of closeness and a 'Foreverness' making all the mud we walked through feel less slippery as our toes gently touched the soft fragrant petals. We began to skip faster and faster until it became a race. There was no way to keep up and with a leap of faith my arms let go and closely and carefully watched as the Wisdom Auditor spun out of control. The dizziness was exhausting and all too familiar. The dream was never ending and finding Wisdom Auditor was becoming easier.

VERBA IPSISSIMA

The very words.

Four

BURNING BRAIN

"Emptiness here, Emptiness there, but the infinite universe stands always before your eyes" —Sengstan third Zen Patriarch

The Water is lap, lap, lapping against the side of the hull. The taste of fear is on my lips.

"What is this great accomplishment moving you so swiftly to search for peace?" spoke the Wisdom Auditor.

Quickly my voice chanted, "Oh Wisdom Auditor, when everything is taken away from you there is nothing to be attached to. With new eyes you simply allow things to be. This is my 'as above so below.'"

"My Dearest, how many times do you think the flesh is considered the Divine body and how many words are spoken knowing this as the truth? After all breaths have been taken the intention is still there. The world will still compete for your attention. The distinction between thoughts will remain and they will always be your own. What can never be taken away is the gift of the heart."

As those final words were spoken, the Wisdom Auditor indulged me with a sense of purity and confidence. The feeling of raptured love encased me.

When my previous suitor came to call he brought me manna and offered the gift of his evil friendship. My life was very simple and the Golden Rule had been tattooed long before this birth time. The best one could offer was in the sharing of the precious gift known as time. Learning to trust was now the unspoken matrix of emotion.

Second chances are the miracles generating wisdom. When nature allows for a breath to be shared with another soul it can only be described in human words as love. Would love surpass all randomness or would it create a space inside the vacuum which held not only my records but without doubt those of another?

How could falling in love be heard when the heart can barely hear a whisper, let alone the cooing from a Dove?

Could there be love without suffering? What is the meaning of love without suffering?

"Wisdom Auditor, why do you persist in staying by my side? Have you anywhere else to attend?"

He replied ever so present, *"No, not at this time my lovely one you are my cause and purpose. For this reason we will share and make certain every opportunity is available to you for examination and the release will be made."*

He repeated, *"Please remember, suffering is the agent of ignorance. When you reach deep inside your core and realize there is no gain or loss the moment will cease to exist as you thought. Those fleeting glances into pain will fail to remain at the scene. Now my precious lovely, let's get on with it. Close your eyes for there is a place you need to be."*

My body sank into a chair not there before.

My mind was racing and there was no rational conclusion. Nothing could ever make sense of this benign insanity. The question screamed from my lips, "Why? Was not the gift of such a divine love worthy of 'Foreverness'?"

The window sill was covered with tiny glass vessels. Crystal clear reminders of how our life was saturated with a sharing created long before our bodies met. We stood face-to-face monitoring our obsession with one another.

Re-defining the object of love by creating a treaty signified by elemental gesture ...we collected salt shakers.

It appeared this was a silly yet mindful prank between us and these mini tokens were simply a gesture of love. It was all deemed perfect. Old and even older were our minds together. Painful memories of being uninvited to the event no longer shadowed my heart. Maidens who had taken the journey dressed me in the orange organza robes made for Goddesses. This invitation sparkled with golden orbs and led me to drink from the chalice. There was no Alice in Wonderland to haunt my response to this appointed investiture.

The grass was wet and the urgency was contained with perfect rhythm. Our beings co-existed with a destiny only "Aida" would surpass. She would be the taker and keeper of my love.

The relentless attempts to keep this 'Foreverness' were known to both of us. Something calls you to the greater cause and the harbinger cannot be ignored.

The faint scent of those Forget-me-nots waffled as the Wisdom Auditor sat with his knees touching mine as we were airlifted to an intersection filled with cars and buses. My curiosity was never-ending and another question was always percolating. "Please tell me about illusions".

Was this my imagination or was my heart fully weakened by the heart of another? Did this man, who held my attention and burned my brain with insatiable adoration, bordering on lust, really exist? Did the ludicrous really need to happen for life to be explained again? We sat together as my eyes fell heavy and the aroma of this floral bouquet called love petitioned me to awaken.

This part of my life is forever burned into the cycle of reality.

It was an unusually cold Saturday morning in January and my regular visit to the restored Court House turned Library once again proved to be most successful. There was always a book waving its hands gifting me with hours and hours of blissful dreamy pleasure. The Library was a circus for my mind. If not three at least four days excluding weekends one would find me sitting at the long tables inhaling everything previously thought and thoughtfully recollected. If reading was an addiction there was never going to be a cure for me. It was difficult to know what olfactory would have to do with it but the moment those massive twenty foot doors opened there was something hallucinatory about the smells that lured me up the massive marble and granite winding staircase. The shelves were crammed with leather bound books carrying the scent of fingers from the one who had previously caressed their pages. Intense curiosity possessed me, wondering what each person thought as they devoured the pages filled with black ink?

There was another aspect of this ritual that never left me, one planted since sitting in my grade two classroom. Books were lonely. Somehow, feeling them was easy for me. Books were friends without introduction, telling a story existing between a front and back cover. They were captured and held without knowledge of their whereabouts. Books had to trust they were chosen for intelligence, wisdom and a dedication to sharing something new. This was a tall order and in making friends with so many of them at every opportunity, the Library became the most perfect place for me to find contentment in their unconditional friendship.

This was my secret castle, a fortress safely guarded and managed by compassionate Library angels protecting immortal inventory for all of us seekers.

The books were adored and protected with the highest regard for its authors and contributors who spent tireless hours creating legacies and wisdoms to serve humanity. These ageless geniuses poured their imaginations and contemplations onto pages without knowing who would eventually read them. People like me who wished to navigate through life without leaving their chair always found a buried treasure.

My parents never worried when Saturday and Sunday rolled around as they knew exactly where to find me. Often times they would show up unannounced waiting curbside at the Library front door at closing hour offering to drive me home. Otherwise the walk to the bus stop would commence.

When they did pick me up, my father would always ask, "What did you find interesting today?"

For the most part my searches danced between Art and Philosophy, but many times the flirtation of romantic and mysterious authors dotted my table. Studying the images and text generated a ride inside my imagination.

On occasion an extraordinary book would be taken out. Rushing home knowing the pages would be inhaled while holding a flash light under the covers through the wee hours of the morning. My insatiable desire to carry all the books home with me was cured by being given permission to stay as long as needed during each visit.

The special books were constructs for my future revelations. There was no doubt at the age of fourteen my relationship with Jean Paul Sartre and Salvador Dali paved the way for the fieldwork in my personal revolution.

The walk to the bus stop required a detour this particular Saturday afternoon. It was really cold although the sun seemed to mesmerize the chill into a state of warmth blessing my feet. The long walk into the downtown core felt serendipitous. A last minute decision to treat myself to a Laura Secord "Goldie" meant that the bus ride would not happen.

This was where my soul mate chose to meet me.

When we met inside the candy store on King Street, there was no candy, no shelves nothing but two persons standing in an aisle filled with light and a dazzling sense of the "dance".

We both knew there would be a story one day to be told. How brilliant was the purpose of my detour, unknown to one another only to pacify the adoration and love of a simple chocolate-covered caramel. The synchronicities began. In that brief moment we could never have known the depth by which our lives would change.

Inside the store were two customers. Recognizing the charming high school friend who shared a locker next to mine, he introduced his friend. A blinding chemistry created a new element on the periodic table. Have you ever felt instantly old? This was the only way to describe the ageless feeling of a bond already known to have existed. There was a knowing beyond our years along with a sense of sadness. We would never experience longevity. It was most unkind. We exchanged our courtesies and the walk home became the beginning of the infinite Opening of the Wedge. There were no cars, houses, or people only a memory of something beyond familiar which required a deep courage to acknowledge.

A few days after this date with destiny, a phone call affirmed we would meet again. Innocence and naivety ran circles around us. We chose to relinquish what was deemed normal and together created our own childhood. From the extremes of silliness to the epic tragedies of Homer, we built our stories. This was second nature to us as we sat on a bus headed to Toronto, patiently waiting for the ultimate high our pseudo adult brains could endure. A music fest called Beggars Banquet and a magical night listening to jazz by the famed Oscar Peterson.

Music played a big part in the late sixties and early seventies. Old enough to be on the cusp of hippy, young enough to enjoy playful walks in the rain our lives flourished. Angels took detours to be with us.

Time seemed generous and we indulged in creative spontaneous, mystical love. Every song written was for us, by those who could only dream of being us.

Lurking inside his dream portfolio was a notion to experience life on the high seas. This was not only necessary it became a calling. In a heartbeat the decision was made and the charmer who introduced my soul mate would now join him on a whimsical journey. Several months passed and in between finishing our last year of high school and taking on part-time jobs, we went about life as usual. When enough money was saved the two young friends manifested their critical path and prepared themselves to hop a plane to Florida. By April a boat was secured and purchased; she was named the Aida. She needed much work it was a labor of love for the two who had dreamt of freedom and an (once-in-a-lifetime) adventure.

Christmas promised to be spectacular and filled with loving memories. To my surprise, he had cleverly designed and crafted something personal, but in hind sight it was a metaphor for the future.

The paint had been dripped and rolled evenly inside the majestic decanter and was covered in symbolic labels. Carefully installed on the mouth of the glass piece was a yellow light bulb. It was a handmade lamp and wrapped around the neck was a little green box. Excited by the painstaking effort made by my alter ego my fingers were delighting in the possibility of being presented with a ring. We had seen our high school days together and the promise of a future seemed real.

He asked that the gift be opened in front of my parents. The little green box revealed a gold band with the face of the most elegant woman, the Cameo Lady.

Looking up at my Knight in shining armor, there was a promise fulfilled. It must have taken centuries to be realized. We had fast-forwarded and met each other once again at the precipice of the Opening of the Wedge.

We said nothing. The ring created a moment of dark silence and the bond between us revealed the illusive truth about life. People create their reality and decide what stays in and out of Pandora's Box. There was a destiny for all of us including the Cameo Lady.

To ensure we would have a permanent fond memory the evening before he left, we prepared an unspoken agenda. It held the ceremonial elements of a Broadway production. Looking back there was a looming uncertainty we might not ever see one another again if nature played her vicious hand or if the heart broke while being examined.

We dined at our favorite restaurant with eyes locked on each other in a harmonic convergence. We were in a dance with no music, beginning or end. We existed in the fullness of whom we were and who we would never become.

Our together was now dealt the hand of fate and it churned inside my stomach as the memories of our 'Foreverness" would lie inside of Pandora's Box. We gracefully acknowledged how strange it felt to have known this kind of love. Our hearts were known too well to one another. We would always be two children who chose freedom as the purpose and impermanence as the voice of change.

With innocence, we fell under the spell of ' Foreverness' once more. We then placed the wooden rings on our fingers. With silent ceremony my hand slipped the tiny wooden ring on his finger and we both blushed with awkward smiles. The hope was Mother Nature would intervene if necessary, and keep him alive and take all others hostage. It was a bet and would never come to fruition. We sat in the backseat of his "56 Chevy" our hands gripped tightly staring into the abyss. It was the revelation of life and death. All had been revealed to us. The infinite skies looked down upon us. We became two particles of stardust challenged by the vibration of our hearts. Lifetimes had been lived in order to find one another only to let each go. Our childhood ways were now being buried.

We caught a glimpse of where the ocean would hold my tears and lock them away. This was a place generating a graveyard of mud and we together planted a lotus seed. We chose to believe the wooden rings would float. We would always find one another.

Saltwater keeps everything from drowning. There was excitement stirring within both of us. How incredible to be given an opportunity of realizing a life-long dream. This was a dream others write about without the experience.

We were two fragile people who desired for each to live without regret. Yes, there was risk. When you tangle with intuition you can be bit badly. Eventually we would be a couple, with children and a white picket fence around our home. When "Aida" my lovely temptress came a calling my only hope was in the belief she would protect my Beloved. What she could never become was his wife. In that knowledge she became less my enemy and more the mistress who would always steal, but never own.

She lied to me. Was there a promise or did the illusion of this delusion create a destination there was no returning from? The most heartfelt goodbye sitting in the back of the turquoise blue and white Chevy became the evidence of all things lost. The engine panted and the last breath we could share was taken. He handed me a card in an olive green envelope. The outside was hand-written and addressed to Cara Mia, the name he lovingly pinned on me. The inside said, "Auf Wiedersehen ", and a young thin girl stood wearing dark hose, her head hanging below her shoulders with stringy brown hair with tears falling. The image was shocking and my initial reaction was one of intense grief. She was the harbinger of what would become my image.

The words were written with salted tears in his handwriting "Keep a light burning in your heart and in your window, I love you Cara Mia."

We made a promise the rings would serve as reminders of our love and friendship and if necessary would keep him afloat should the waters decide to hold him down.

We drove home with nervous energy and lived a century in thought. Our hands were folded and locked in a slip knot. My grief began during our drive on the silent road. The lights became the tunnel as the etheric cross became heavier to carry every second forward.

In the knowing one learns the details of suffering. She is not my friend nor is she my enemy.

With great hesitation and after an hour of begging, my weakness for him got the better of me. The decision was made we would rendezvous one last time before he escaped to meet Aida. There was no doubt taking my time was necessary, and the walk seemed endless and almost cruel. Gathering all my courage and trying desperately to build a wall of protection around myself the front door opened. It was inevitable but our chemistry was no match for the blasé world existing outside.

We moved between realities and time. Our bodies locked and the igniting began.

As the wicked arm of Thor and the most powerful current wiped us out, we stood inside a vortex pushing us backward unable to stand upright.

We glared at each other and then started laughing hysterically feeling the electrical aftermath.

The Grim Reaper closed the door behind me and began preparing me for the final chapter. My heart kidnapped itself and held no ransom. There was no looking back for fear he would be looking at me and create a greater casualty.

It seems irrational to have experienced this depth of the heart at such a young age. Shakespeare wrote of this intensity and in the final chapter of Romeo and Juliet we discover pain and the source of retrieving the messages implanted in the heart. In the days following, the reality of never growing old together became a distinct possibility. Months passed and the few letters received were always filled with love for me and a passion for his mistress "Aida". She was being prepared for her maiden journey. We spoke to one another the night before they set sail. His voice was imbued with a somber tone and while we spoke my eyes were glued to the inside of the beautiful glass lamp he had painstakingly made for me. The paint drippings began to look like colored tears. It struck me he had not put a sailboat inside rather he created a wave that seemed to thrash from one side to the other. The wall of glass was weakening. There was a strong and undeniable sense of fear in his childlike voice yet neither one of us spoke about it.

The Aida was now seaworthy and the decision to sail her for an indefinite period of time had been made.

My heart had prepared for this and without sharing, the release was made. The days were now silent and lonely. The decision to let go of this foolish pirate who was living his dream seemed to be the only anchor for my sanity. Surrendering to Aida who knowingly shared his destiny was the only way of rationalizing my future.

Eventually, the emptiness was filled with human tenderness. Comfort was not an excuse for love yet it was a distraction and a confirmation of existing. Content to relax without knowledge of the pirates dream seemed to make life more palatable.

Months had gone by and finally a letter written by him arrived. There was hesitation in my desire to open the envelope and read the haunting words. They were written with a dark and ominous ink, somewhat prophetic and charged with a potent poison. The letter had been constructed carefully and mindfully with a tenderness leaving me to feel his absolute absence. There were three pages filled with news and one poem he created. Three lines stood out and became a mantra tattooed permanently in my psyche.

"The taste of fear is on my lips. The Water is lap, lap, lapping against the side of the hull, I will always love you…my Cara Mia."

The letter was folded and put away. A few days later, my father called on a Wednesday afternoon, informing me he would be coming to visit later that evening. This was quite out of the ordinary as it was a midweek trip well over sixty miles one way.

At first my initial thought was something horrible had happened to someone in our family and he was going to share this news. We were close knit and our feelings were most often expressed when we were together, not on the phone.

For this reason, there was a preciousness flirting with already scripted words. My mind was figuring out what comfort would be offered to him.

This was a command performance and the adaptation was critically acclaimed by the rulers of heaven. My father delivered a soliloquy leaving the curtain down never to be opened for an encore. His biting words were surreal "he's gone." The chamber of my heart watched the wooden ring slowly sink to the bottom.

The words were screams and every salt shaker sitting on the window sill of my childhood room burst into a sea of damnation. My soul mate had taken a journey and Aida had not protected him. His fate was presumed by drowning while on watch during the night. Why? Why?

Remember suffering is only in the details.

The information was scarce which made it even more difficult to comprehend. The waters were reasonable, but perhaps not? As told in the hours to follow, he was without a life line and Aida became difficult to control during his watch.

The Aida did not protect him and the boom shaft denied him safety. Our families mourned and my heart was now forever going to be under examination. The following days were filled with a lifelessness that succumbed to dire states of grief and a darkness preparing me for future losses and heart ache.

Life did hold a grand purpose and without question all karma would unfold as it was supposed to.

"Wisdom Auditor, have you seen him? Does he have a precious new soul?" The heavens must have embraced him. Do you think he will ever find me again?

My mind and heart would believe it to be true. He now prepares the work necessary in order to find me again.

The tragic loss of a childhood sweetheart parallels to the innocence lost when the uninvited use their weak Tiger Blood to hunt. For years, the question lingered until the resolve was made five years later when the death of my father revived my faith in humanity and the purpose of our existence. My brain burned with anger and emptiness. The basis for all rationale is change. It must be. It cannot stop itself. Why do we persist in static living?

Why does it hurt so deeply in the guts of confusion and the persistence of curiosity?

"Wisdom Auditor, when will this make sense?"

"My lovely one, he was here for an eternity and in between the breath you found one another. Aida was the sailing ship to his next journey. You must be grateful as you were able to churn the waters under the milky sea for him. All the demons were aroused by your considerations for one another, but they chose him."

"Perhaps, because he was so loved by you, they found him worthy."

Wisdom Auditor put his arms around me and for the first time my mind stopped burning.

Cleaning out a drawer, approximately a year later, a tiny little scratch pad was found. Opening it to the first page, the words "Remember Me Day" were written in his handwriting.

Five

TRANSPARENT FORGIVENESS

Wisdom Auditor held my gaze and very slowly my body relaxed and sleep converted my rage to rest. During this time my lovely one called upon me and requested with such a pleasurable voice, *"You must always remember you are never alone."*

When the door closed, my head was swimming under water and the only recollection of prior was when my body was lifted to safety. Wisdom Auditor was standing above me gazing into my golden eyes. A smile surfaced between us and the knowing proclaimed our oneness. *"Let me carry you forward. With all the families waiting, you may claim your position."* What intrigue and caring. The wheelchair arrived and there he sat without blinking on the cold and flat leather seat. This was not a dream. There was no karmic alibi here.

After completing the circuit of a typical teenage summer, the bells were ringing again for the start of another school year.

It was September, and the glory of experiencing life away from the city was once again a bonus. Every weekend up north was further enhanced by being with those who made a wonderful difference in our lives.

The family greeted us with patience, knowing that we would consume their house and time. Hours were spent cruising through town to secret creeks, waterfalls, and magical forests, blaring 'Radar Love'. This detour became the reward after a hard week working in the concrete jungle. This particular weekend tightened all reasons for one family to stand together. If faith had a name it was going to reveal itself.

The family attended a typical country wedding where the entire clan reveled in revisiting with those who had not been seen for a very long time. Everyone was there to enjoy the sharing of baby photos, clinking glasses, begging and screaming for the bride and groom to kiss.

The dance floor recalled the autograph of each shoe leaving its imprint during the stomping of the wild and ridiculous songs from years gone by without knowledge there had been a dance for life held down the road. While this party was taking place one family member decided to stay back with a friend after work. My brother-in law might join us later. That's what teenagers do, as they find their freedom. With school commencing around the corner it was the last weekend hurrah and spending it with your parents was least likely to get the vote.

Choice and destiny took control.

My brother-in-law sat in the passenger seat of a pickup truck with an empty load, on his way home after one of the last days of his summer employment. He was probably thinking about the weekend ahead and it was obvious he was not interested in finding us at the wedding.

Driving through the barren, winding roads of cut rock and narrow pathways the rain was beating down on the windshield. The roads were slick and reminiscent of black ice. The back end of the truck lost gravity and control. The vehicle skidded to the edge of the road and plummeted over the cliff into the cold water of the lake, without mercy crushing my brother-in law's body under its weight. He was pinned against the door.

The driver was able to free himself and quickly realized his passenger was unable to move. Working frantically he pulled him out of the truck now filling up with water. His body was dragged to the road.

It was now after three a.m. and the pounding on the door was relentless. My eyes opened irritated by the constant flashing through the window. It was apparent the light source was sitting on top of a police car. My father-in-law opened the door to this unlikely guest and listened intently to the guided words of the Officer who was known to them.

There had been an accident involving my brother-in-law. If the eyes of my father-in-law could speak there would be a new note on the harmonic scale. We gathered at the kitchen table as he tried to make sense of the news he had just received. With a shaken voice he guided us through the unimaginable. My brother-in-law sustained significant injury and was now being air-lifted to a hospital in Toronto.

It was a deer-in-the-headlights moment for each of us as we gasped and realized the noise we heard overhead was more than likely the Medevac helicopter carrying him. We scurried to gather our belongings and headed straight for our cars and the long three-hour drive to Toronto.

Time is like a vacuum cleaner; it gifts you with a tool to clean up a mess, but once it inhales there is no place to hide; it still exists, but in a different form. It is now out of sight and yet always in existence. The drive was like that. Repetitive words playing over and over like hitting a tilt knob on a pin ball machine. Arriving at the hospital could not have happened fast enough.

Along the side rail of the steel frame bed stood my then husband and father-in-law, neither one capable of speaking.

The young man covered in dirt and stones kept his eyes closed. We stood next to the bed waiting for him to move. It did not happen.

"Have you an answer?" we asked the doctors who stood by with large black X-Rays that had obviously been examined as there were white marks over them. We were guided to a light box and the X-Rays were carefully mounted. A mumbling took place and very few sentences made sense, yet the final words were more than clear. "His spinal cord has been severed and he will most likely not regain the use of his arms or legs. He will be a quadriplegic."

My heart sank as the shock of these words collapsed inside my head. There was a deafening silence as the words echoed. It was an unacceptable statement and one never to be believed. Something will change and his prognosis would be much different.

The next moment created the deepest dilemma for my then father-in-law. He was the one who would go back into the room and inform his second eldest son what the doctor had told us.

We had been given the Requiem to a never ending Mass.

At seventeen, this was not a death sentence, rather a curse, from a hell realm no one should ever experience. How does one justify a punishment of this enormity when a crime was never committed or given a proper trial?

Wisdom Auditor motioned for me to join him away from the others. There was a chapel down the hall and we entered it together. The room was dark with stain glass windows highlighted by a faux box light. It made the red glass look like blood stains and my eyes darted away from it.

Not wishing to cry any longer, my head fell onto the shoulder of the Wisdom Auditor. *"You have the answer in the questions you have asked. If you know how to ask these, you already know how to find the answers."*

The room was spinning and the notion of loneliness swept through me. It disguises itself in many ways, but it never hesitates to be seen in the face of others. Perhaps this was one of the answers.

The life he had now created was to be made whole. If there are words to describe the macabre they were now part of our daily vocabulary.

Aida had crossed the cold water, this time she did not claim her victim.

Life does have a purpose and all notion of desperation was shelved and only hope replaced the inevitable trials of the future. The questions never left my heart and the answers were spontaneous, yet never satisfactory. For months and months powerful forces worked to invigorate his attitude and muscles. At the rehabilitation hospital hope came when spasms began to painfully ignite. Learning to live with these limitations and an uncertain future took its toll. There was a suffering and sadness felt by all of us, this was not just his battle to conquer. It was shared equally by everyone in his life.

My renegade vision was to see him live life fully drunk on the cocktail of normal existence. As years passed he redefined his life and had many successes. To observe his stamina and willingness to fight throughout his life altered my perspective on reality.

No one should tell another person's story and for all good reasons. Perceptions are churned out with selfish agendas; metaphors created to pacify the outcomes, but if one can learn from the lesson alone it is worth the price of admission. The attempt to create and hold the space for his suffering changed my life forever. What became crystal clear is without seeing or questioning suffering one cannot measure the value of life.

Wisdom Auditor smiled and beckoned me back to the room where there were no glass walls. *"Have you ever wondered what phenomena means?"* Judging that this was going to take me to a place of discomfort my knee jerk reaction was to answer immediately; to quickly end this conversation. This was exactly what should happen. The truth in the reality of life is it is ineffable only revealed to us when we place our minds in the clarity of NOW.

All things were phenomena to me. Each breath taken was considered miraculous. All persons who were part of my journey were not occupational hazards. The universe controls phenomena and in these relationships we find our wisdom teachers. He had become one of mine. There is a bar code with an expiry date in our DNA according to the unresolved and yet to be decoded human genome.

"The greatest source of inspiration comes to us when we let go of our little dramas and see outside of ourselves."

My head nodded in agreement.

◆◆◆

**"When you lose,
do not lose the lesson."**

—His Holiness the 14th Dalai Lama

Six

WARRIOR HIGHWAY

When my eyes screamed to open they were met with blindness. There was no evidence of life or light, only a silent web of darkness. Grasping to feel the re-birth of my mind and body the struggle was relentless. The painful "blur" began with a drowning sensation of bubbles and robotic circuits being activated.

The pain ripped and tore through my head and was exacting. Starting at the crown it felt like a hammer hitting an anvil with an electric drill pulsating at warp speed. The precision of awareness was daunting as this became the moment of being brought back to life, again. Caught in a state of suspension for quite some time the fact remained, this had been my choice to play the hand of fate in the game of Russian roulette. This was a state of being in between cause and effect. Until death arrives we live by caring for ourselves with incredible dedication. For certain, we assume each day will arrive preparing us for the next and the next. On this day, my fate resulted in a miracle and a relationship with the Wisdom Auditor.

It was late in the summer of 1976 and for a few short years we lived in the beautiful heart of the Canadian prairies in the province of Saskatchewan.

It was a Saturday morning and through the windows of our tiny little castle, the sun was blinding and brilliant. The air was clean and crisp, yet there was a definite strange predictive feeling that loomed.

Living in a small town with a population of less than 300 inhabitants you quickly developed uncommon friendships and an unspoken sense of family. Living in this breathtaking part of Canada one had the ability to traverse the country roads and watch wild horses overtake unclaimed lands. Sitting on sand dunes feeling the Prairie desert air caress the face was innocence personified.

Often, we would patiently listen to the unmistakable, swooshing sounds of the precious wheat fields chattering in perfect harmony with all of nature. This was an irreplaceable gift one should call true bliss. Every day became a new and Godly experience. Winter days postured themselves with snowmobiling off rooftops of houses covered by massive amounts of snow fall. We would see ninety days of minus forty-degree temperatures. In contrast, summer days begged for one to stand still and just gaze in awe at the landscape melting into patterns of sacred geometry. There were days when synesthesia moments took place. You could feel the colors and sounds as if they were sent down by the angels in a Divine musical composition beckoning for your approval and attention.

Rural towns have their own unique lifestyle. Friends drop by routinely unannounced. It was not unusual to receive guests riding up to your front door on their four-hoofed vehicle of choice. Many lazy hours were spent playing guitars on the lawn with neighbors joining in to share the limelight. This particular Saturday was no different except for one brief moment which in retrospect has become my date with destiny on the "Warrior Highway".

One of our friends arrived in town riding his majestic part Quarter, part Appaloosa horse. Listening to the unmistakable sound of its hooves lured me to peek out the living room window. The sight of this enormous and breathtaking animal completely overtook my senses. My only thought was what a thrill it would be to ride this magnificent creature, feel its power and conquer a winding path through town! This is where all logic and sensibility dissolved on the playing field of karma. At the age of twenty-two my judgment was deemed unusually mature.

Seemingly confident and routinely cautious one would consider me a non-risk taker. Endangerment of life, especially my own, would never be a consideration or thought in good conscience.

My mode of transportation was a CJ5 Golden Rod Jeep with canvas roof and doors, which was driven an average of forty five miles in one direction on both highway and grid roads to and from my job daily. During the winter my body was kept from freezing to death with a warm wolf pelt coat. It never crossed my mind this beautiful four-legged angelic animal would be any more challenging than changing gears in my jeep.

With a grin on my face like a Cheshire cat, my body waltzed over and ever so meekly and politely the "ask" was made. "Would it be okay for me to hop onto this lovely creature for a short little ride through the neighborhood?" Without missing a beat, he said, "Sure honey, you obviously know how to ride?" The distance between yes and no "in an innocent white lie" spawned further than the distance between the sun and the Milky Way. Without hesitation a very big grin crossed my face!

My then husband stared at me in disbelief as he echoed in slow motion, "You don't know how to ride!" His words were numb to my ears and discarded into the air.

Quickly, my mind slipped back to a time in high school when a group of us hitch-hiked to a farm in the countryside and spent a dollar and fifty cents for three hours of guilt-free pleasure riding in a pasture. It was true my horse was older and slower. The guide constantly needed to prod my little filly to keep up with the others.

The vision confirmed my abilities and my voice resonated with a confident "Yes!" Clearly some experience was under my belt and there was no reason this should not be a similar auspicious, unremarkable and memorable event.

So began the next karmic alibi.

Barely weighing one hundred pounds, assistance was given to lifting my frame up to the saddle and the sensation of power overwhelmed all my senses. Fear was not an option and together in harmony we began our date with destiny.

Our first one-hundred feet seemed perfect as we moved at a very comfortable and even slow pace. This epic and Olympic-defined event was not a challenge and was flawlessly executed. My body began to relax and ever so quietly under my breath the words "Vive Horsewoman Extraordinaire!" were whispered. This however was a short-lived acclaim as seconds later something went terribly wrong. To this day, like a roll of cellophane film, the event will repeat over and over in my head as there is no way of knowing what triggered the spooking of this horse. Perhaps it had figured out the creature on its back was incredibly naive and untrained. What seemed perfectly benign had now turned into a race against time, space and possible death. Mine.

Both of us began to panic and control over the situation was no longer in the equation. The strong legs were pounding the unpaved dirt road as it filtered between all obstacles in its path. My hands gripped the reigns, believing when we reached the end of the main street, logic would prevail and waltzing comfortably through the piazza would take place. The pace continued to escalate until we reached the edge of town and the longest stretch of the world lay before me. It was the TransCanada highway now unveiling a new definition of shock and fear.

These were not just emotions they were evidence of impermanence.

I glanced to the left and right, all the while believing this treasured animal would realize it was far from its home and simply give way to slowing down. This ticket to Paradise had been bought by my foolish, impatient and inconsiderate need for a Saturday morning thrill. Even with my snake charming skills, there was no potion. The ability to cast a spell was useless as the Abracadabra fell upon deaf ears. There was zero communication between the two of us.

We turned right onto the highway in the probable direction of where the farm and stable might be.

My assumption regarding panic was correct. We would pound pavement very hard with an unknown destination perhaps two maybe seven miles away. There was a competition between logic and insanity going on inside my head, as we engaged the race down the earth's longest racetrack. The movie Gladiator did not come close to what was happening in my arena.

It is said, when you sense death is imminent scenes from your life flash before you.

In this instance at the ripe old age of twenty-two there were definitely marked experiences, yet none more significant than the one before me. Nothing could have prepared me for what was about to happen next.

The decision to get on the horse was no longer important. My life was now in the hands of the Warrior Highway. In hindsight what was so necessary for me to take such risk with so little respect for myself and my precious life?

It ran deeper than just a joy ride. It was my own delusion, and the only alibi was my mind must have evaporated.

The wind was blowing madly through my hair. Remaining rational compromised my senses. All good thoughts were screaming out of control along with my blaring voice until silence arrived.

Travelling at warp speed my attempt to whisper frantically into its ears proved completely futile. Armageddon was manifesting.

At this point, it did not matter as we were galloping full tilt on the TransCanada Highway with no evidence of coming to a stop. Would my body survive the wicked cement surprise? It had been recorded the fastest horse on earth clocked in at a frightening fifty-miles-per-hour. With the pedigree of my beast, there was no doubt we were travelling well over forty. The conversation played out in my head would probably have made Saturday Night Live seem like a scene from Captain Kangaroo. Knowing this was as close to entering the Twilight Zone as one would ever get, all options were being calculated and the revisions were not favorable.

If there was a Supreme Being it was now time to show up, and get this situation under control. Please make yourself known to me, and if you are too busy…send your boss!

My words were innocently desperate as they twirled around in the unknown space.

"Forgive me for being an arrogant, egotistical, immature showoff… blah blah…. without license to ride!" Actually, those were not the exact words ... it was more like "What the blank was in your head you ditzy shoulder-padded bimbo blond?"

Was this the Opening of the Wedge?

Easily compared to watching an epic film where you anxiously await with baited breathe to find out what the hero or heroine will choose to do, believing in your heart you know the favorable one. Fear was the only truth residing as this scene predicted a less than favorable outcome.

Close your eyes and try to remember a time when you lifted your face up to the skies as the rain fell. Remember the warmth of the gentle and wet beads caressing your cheeks as the tiny droplets dripped from your eyelashes making your eyes flutter and your heart beat a little quicker. This might have been a wonderful description of my predicament if described by the imagination of a romantic poet. However it was not a romantic scene in a movie and my imagination had already drowned in the plethora of fear it had been feeding on for the past one hundred seconds.

Options were growing scarce. The gobs of liquid flowing from the mouth of this scared and frothing animal were slapping my cheeks and hair, blinding my eyes. The beating of my heart could be heard in China or mistaken for the mistral winds in the south of France.

The idea of experiencing a major heart attack followed by imminent death seemed a much painless fate.

Becoming bedfellows with the oncoming transport truck crushed my belief that survival was an option. My mind raced to camouflage that image, allowing me to become a glorious Matador in a Spanish arena calculating my escape. A thought occurred to me, I don't even know the name of my partner in crime. Could it be Warrior or Serendipity? We had just met and not properly introduced. This was a blind date.

There is no relationship between us, my voice weakened as tears mixed with froth pelted. My heart wept for the possible death of two strangers destined for the after-life together.

Heaven forbid its heart failed or it simply decided to stop abruptly catapulting me hundreds of feet in the air to meet the cement pavement without a proper greeting. Facing the front of the transport truck inching closer and closer in the oncoming lane forced my decision.

The karmic alibi began to develop. Was this really happening to me or was this a moment in someone else's living-room being replayed for my observation? When does a dream become reality? Fighting to stay alive all negative thoughts were crushed as death was not going to be an option. My brain was hard-wired into the CIA and FBI of life. There had to be an immediate solution. What would James Bond do? What brilliant exit strategy would he have engineered? The reality set in, "You are not James Bond and there will not be a Knight in shining armor strategically parking his helicopter on the side of the TransCanada Highway, preparing to throw you a lifeline and carry you off to safety." The outcome was becoming more and more frightening.

My decision to risk dying in order to save myself could be seen as heroic and accidental yet seemed suicidal. If my life was spared would it be called an unfortunate accident? Sadly, the vision of my mangled and unrecognizable body flashed before me. The thought of living the rest of my life in a wheelchair was an all too familiar reality and would never be tolerated.

If death resulted, no single person would ever know the truth or understand it was not an intentional taking of life, rather a leap of faith to survive.

There were no words to describe the degree of insanity waxing and waning through my mind. The depth of loneliness was unparalleled to any depression, fatigue or anxiety the mind could cultivate. Those were conjured emotions similar to self-inflicted addictions. My brain was coming to grips with the shortage of time and a decision would have to be made before one was made for me. Desperately, my mind tried to organize all brain cells and circuits to become rationale and calm. The realization a violent death could happen increased the panic within. If this animal opted to remove me from its back, chances of survival were parallel to the choice needed to be made.

Does one hang in until the options expire? Might we possibly reach the destination of choice and be welcomed by the crowd at the corral gates? The anguish was pitiful and horrified all my senses as we were both out of control. The decision was made. My body would slide off the back of the horse onto the TransCanada Highway at forty miles per hour. It was time inside of time and only the heavens and hells were present making sure there was a distinction.

No amount of imagination could reveal the terror frozen over my face. If forgiveness owned a smile, there may have been one for a brief second. Whatever destiny had in store would now be received with a gasp of humility. The decision seemed daunting and yet there was a stillness that set in, a sense of pure peace.

How does one who loves life inhaling every second now imagine the door of fate opening forcing you to walk through?

The reigns slacked from my frigid and panicked hands and my mouth softly kissed the neck of the beast while my lips begged for forgiveness whether deserved or not.

In the fullness of time my voice fell still and whispered, "Please God, Christ, Buddha and Bahaullah embrace and forgive me." The reigns slowly slipped thru my fingers and without any further hesitation my body followed, slithering hastily down between the thundering hooves. My rare and perfect life ended as it met the arrogant darkness of death.

◆◆◆

"Mind is the builder."

—Edgar Cayce

Seven

KARMIC DEADLINE

Wisdom Auditor smiled at me with a grin leading me to believe he found my experience to be somewhat victorious.

There was a cementing of knowledge without words and the relationship with Wisdom Auditor felt familiar and very much needed.

What shall we do now? Wisdom Auditor offered his hand and without hesitation our fingers locked and we started to walk. There was a natural and spontaneous gait that flowed between us, so perfect, so flawless.

There was a hint this experience was neither going to be joyful or unpleasant. What should have been confusing and deliberate appeared effortless and necessary.

"Do you know what imagination is?" asked the Wisdom Auditor.

"Yes, of course." The feeble words spilled out of my mouth.

"Could you imagine a world where forgiveness would never be necessary, where all actions would be without malice, or intent to cause suffering?"

My head once again felt heavy and my eyes looked briefly up to the sky as it morphed into seven mountains covered in blue snow, surrounded by ancient designs and without cause my body slammed hard into the ground.

The conversation was no longer static, the sentences spoken were rifles of words saturating my mind and the only defense was to lay still and listen. My heart had stopped beating.

My head struggled to reconnect with my body. My vision was completely out of focus. For a brief moment a rainbow glided across my eyelids and tears began to trickle down my cheeks. There was no separation between myself and the river that embraced me.

The flurry of all things past no longer seemed relevant. Everything simply existed without cause. Slowly my head began to lift itself up as if feeling the weight of a one ton boulder. On the ground my shadow was merging as if it had just caught up with me. A reconnection was happening as a life had been spared, or was this lucid and perhaps death?

The delight to find myself alive and breathing shifted quickly to my senses. Each of them reassigned as if they were being introduced for the first time. It appeared all seemed to be functioning ... and a wave of gratitude came over me only to be described as a fractured open wedge.

Determined to gather myself with some sense of dignity, relief came when Wisdom Auditor was spotted sitting on a large rock several feet away. Everything was being made visible and looked familiar, however, the intensity of the pain was gouging, leaving me in a non-existent time zone. Without comprehension of what was taking place, Wisdom Auditor glided over to me.

It felt like morning again.

The ground did not exist; there was no bed or pillow. All that existed seemed to co-exist with this place of no form.

The silence seduced me into exhaustion relaxing into a blissful state of listening. The magic of this possible dream was no longer painful. The magic of this dream was no longer feared. It was now peaceful by design and contemplative without curiosity.

There was an etheric sense of trust. A voice began to speak. *"Do you wake up every morning believing you have a fortunate life?"* My mind ran in every direction as it jolted itself trying to piece together an answer. Thinking was excruciating and difficult at best. There was no imminent threat here, although the desire to give the right answer was more than provocative. The relentless questions continued bordering on unnerving. The dirt had birthed a new blossom filled with mystery and seduction.

The words were irrelevant as my creation was now in the integrity of protective forces. All circumstances were favorable and my heart orchestrated a gratification of simply being in awe of this extra-ordinary experience. Wisdom Auditor sat quietly observing without judgment letting me bathe in the conception of transformation. With silence and without measure, projecting or creating the weight of my suffering began to cease.

Wisdom Auditor handed me a Golden feather.

My fingers gently lifted the feather toward my face embracing the cashmere softness with a knowing this was the beginning of another path. There was no escape from the commitment to accept life. Realizing everyone we meet in life is there by circumstance of birth or intentionally invited. This was no longer about choice as decisions made long ago were catching up. With a glint of satisfaction he offered his hand and another walk began. *"Do you desire freedom? If so, walk through the door with me."*

This was the gift of another NOW.

Wisdom Auditor stood nearby and watched as the car my then husband was driving inched along the shoulder looking for evidence of my body. It was difficult to determine how much time had passed since the decision to save myself.

Awakening was extremely painful. Voices sounded like relentless Hi Hat drums, and words were foreign, making no sense, similar to the Tower of Babylon. There was nothing comprehensible coming out of his mouth and it aggravated me immensely. There was intense body pain and total confusion inside my head. The trauma of being kicked by the horse then hitting the pavement was a violent assault. The jolt felt by hitting the highway was like a vapor mist, as if it had not even taken place. What became horribly obvious was "a death" had occurred and in this realization my mind engaged a new awareness. A battle was taking place to release the confusion and replace it with logic and clarity to resolve in composure and a silent victory.

In fleeting silence there was aloneness, and an urgency to dwarf the intoxicating calmness. My feelings could not be masked.

This became a critical mass building toward a guttural explosion to scream, fight and claw my way out in a warrior stance. Excruciating yet beautiful as death ended and life began again. The heaviness inside my head caused both shoulders to buckle and my body fell limp. Dizziness succumbed and there was a beacon of light swallowing each cell inside completely blinding me.

There were crazy noises and the striations of light in a myriad of color flashed non-stop as everything began to sort out and find its proper place. Concentration became intense. Perhaps in many ways this is evidence of the training ground for my meditation practice. This was a place that heralded realizations in a symphony of cacophony and comedy.

The thickness in my voice was audible inside my head. Feeling this was an illusion, fear began to investigate and for many long hours my rational thinking came to an intentional halt.

A conversation with my then husband never began or ended. If there were words spoken they were immediately discarded and only added an intolerable layer of complexity.

Profound sadness and a relentless stirring of shame brewed inside of me. Ashamed of the decision to expose myself to harm and suffering brought many hours of prolonged silence. The intense embarrassment was never analyzed or shared over tea. It simply became part of my authentic being.

Here was a glimpse into the cycle of life and a belief those harbingers who understood redemption died with a proclamation for our souls. Indeed mine had been touched.

Clearly every breath should not be taken for granted.

My body was carefully lifted into the vehicle. The ride to the hospital was magical as there was an absence of past, present and future. Inside my own imagination an alibi was no longer necessary. Whatever was needed in this one lifetime to reach beyond all those little dramas and 'what if' questions, had now been revealed with clarity and precision.

The school of emptiness had opened its doors for me to walk through, and my feet followed.

The hospital was an unkind place. Maybe it was an inconvenient time to be taken. Were lunches and breaks now being interrupted?

At the emergency entrance there was a nurse who rallied to put me on a stretcher wheeling me into the examination room to manipulate the body just freed from itself. Would it ever be possible to explain to anyone what had taken place?

My mouth and brain were not in sync although the words were formed there was no ability to reveal them. People who have experienced a stroke often describe something very similar and it is shattering. The caregivers seemed robotic and uncaring creating uneasiness inside of me. Did these people not understand or recognize what had just transpired? My eyes could see inside their hearts. They seemed disinterested in me as a person. They did not know of my life or death dilemma. It finally hit me, this is "cowboy country" and riding horses is usual business from the rodeo to daily life. A horse injury of any kind was routine.

The X-Ray felt like mini bombs pulsating as they moved me into positions only a circus contortionist would be capable of managing. Was every bone in my body broken? It felt that way. Trying to be brave after being so alone on the Warrior highway was like climbing Mt. Everest. Every few minutes there was a welling up of tears and the notion of what being brave meant took on new meaning.

The daunting task of learning how to comfortably breathe again with an appropriate rhythm was a concern.

My heart was beating with double and triple beats as if two people were fighting inside.

Totally exhausted, my head rested on the stretcher and my eyes roamed around the room tortured and restless. Seconds later my focus shifted as there sat the Wisdom Auditor who said nothing. His eyes fixated on me with a powerful and hypnotic gaze that surged with anxiousness. A different kind of pain was overtaking my body. My bones were being fused and pushed back together, and my skin covered with blood no longer burned as harshly. Visible to me alone, were fog-like clouds simmering in the surrounding space, and to this day they have never abandoned me.

Had an angelic healing taken place?

It took months to put the pieces together to rationalize what had transpired. Life permanently altered. How would one ever begin to explain this experience when the reality was hardly comprehensible to me? Only time would reveal its source and purpose. My perception was made relevant and the epiphany revealed a pattern of how to forge ahead, remain focused and humble.

The X-Rays results and physical examination were delivered with straight faces. No single break or fractured bone evidenced, only bruising and soft tissue trauma, nothing remarkable. The surprise was genuine and graciously accepted although the pain racing through my body asked for a more believable diagnosis.

Months later my poor body still looked like a walking zombie. The bruising took a long time to heal but was a cake walk compared to the alternative of death.

This was a miracle, the work of an etheric, angelic operating room with a table surrounded by heavenly beings operating 'systems' beyond our knowledge.

Wisdom Auditor was an intervening angel. What makes this different than a dream?

Grateful for life, my journey continued to spiral and left many more petals of miracles along the way.

There are people who share near-death experiences and describe them with great clarity. They talk about their bodies floating above, as they observe what is taking place. People describe streams of white light dancing around them. My experience did not parallel their words.

There had been a "walk" and a discussion creating a vortex in which my life was cast in Divine wonderment. Trying to find meaningful words only frustrates, as there can never be an adequate description. Perhaps, making up my own word will resolve it for now and that word is "Foreverness."

What imprinted in my heart, by the Grace of God and the cycle of karma, is the ultimate confrontation of reality; by seeing impermanence as the opening wedge to the path. My soul had been given another chance at 'time' which clearly meant previous lives manifested. My assumption there would be a litany of tests yet to come was accurate as there have been many more equally as complex.

If there is evidence on earth that 'we truly are part of a grand Wizardry of Cosmic proportion' then what took place this unpredictable Saturday in a little Saskatchewan town can never be questioned.

A breath of life had been whipped into my lungs and caught me as my lifeless body slammed and tumbled onto the concrete cemetery.

The physical recovery took considerably longer and over the years there were constant reminders carried in a freshness of pain. All of this revealing the root cause from one extraordinary day. The emotional trauma was boxed away and rarely examined or came up for discussion. Finding this emptiness was welcomed; it took the pressure off coming up with new excuses, and in some ways brought me closer to realizing mindfulness.

A year later, the company we worked for transferred us to Winnipeg, Manitoba. There was no doubt our imprint had been cast and would abide in the time capsule of many future conversations. A folklore tale with real life characters was a more fitting description. The effort it took to look back became as painful as the original moment itself although there was a gratefulness that took on new meaning.

Life lessons and insights gained always come with a price. My goal in life was always to help the less fortunate and assist those who had difficulty getting their lives together. It is true for some, resistance never leaves. After all had transpired along my path, resistance weakened and it seemed a new stamina with measurable wisdom had blossomed. Intentions were now being carved out.

My life took on greater meaning although the journey was about to get more and more bumpy. Life is a source of unbelievable joy and trauma punctuated by the moments in between where we make choices to determine what the next twenty four hours will look like. From there on end, it changes the cycle of everyone's twenty-four hours.

This is the spiral of life, time inside of time. Dreaming is finding the magical elixir unveiling the alchemy residing inside each radiant star and secretly divulging a drop of knowledge one at a time.

◆◆◆

"If we could read the secret history of our enemies, we should find in each person's life sorrow and suffering enough to disarm any hostility."

—Henry Wadsworth Longfellow

Eight

SULIRAM

It was the morning of November 3, 1978. The phone rang at 4:44 a.m.

The flight from Winnipeg to Toronto was drenched in rain and tears. My precious father had suffered a massive heart- attack and was on life support. The voice on the other end of the phone whispered "please come home now". In my day to day existence there was a permeable reality. Life had taken me to an event without an invitation, stole my precious childhood love and now the cruelest of all suffering was happening. As the plane landed there was darkness, fear and a miserable reality would soon become another punctuation mark in my calendar.

When my uncle picked me up from the airport he sported a very illegal smile even he had trouble sustaining. He drove me directly to the hospital and there before me was my beautiful father with his amber eyes closed.

My most precious and angelic creator was intubated and lifeless. The Doctor immediately came over stating my father had indeed suffered a massive coronary and was in a coma. He shared there was always a chance he might hear me and be aroused from this dormant state. "Speak to him in a meaningful dialogue. It might be a trigger for him to awaken." He urged me to consider trying. It was difficult to ground myself as only three hours earlier my head was spinning with all of the "what if's."

Remaining composed depleted me. Contemplating all the special treasures we shared only one act would serve its purpose. It wasn't a poem or a line from a book. It was our deep love for music and especially the intoxicating voice of Miriam Makeba. She was a popular South African songstress and humanitarian.

The brilliance of living in a multi-cultural home with a father who had so much appreciation for all ethnicities exposed us to the world beyond our heritage.

My lips quivered and eventually popped open with a very faint and almost squeaky sound. Somehow the voice within managed to reveal itself with the quality of a Prothonetary Fall warbler lost in a swamp far away from home. The song sent shivers through my body and if the walls in the Cardiac I.C.U. could talk they too would be part of this benign concert. My heart wept with each word. "Suliram" is an African lullaby dearly loved by my father. On his fortieth birthday my rendition was gifted to him and from that day forward it became our song.

If my father was going to die, my soul mate taken by the Aida would find him and journey together. It was inevitable he would never open his eyes.

Wisdom Auditor joined me on the edge of the hospital bed,*"Oh, my lovely one, why do you cry?"* Unable to hide my despair he insisted there was nothing but compliance needed. This was evolution and the change maker.

"Why did you not tell me he was going to die?"

On November ninth, precisely at eleven minutes after eleven a.m. my precious father died and his body was gracefully carried by the archangels to heaven.

His eyes were closed and the crisp, dry sheet was pulled over his head. That act felt so merciless. This man should be covered in nothing less than a royal robe.

Looking over at my mother, she stood in what seemed like the middle of an active volcano. There was no way to get inside her head. She was quiet, yet a subtle rage and confusion was seen in her eyes. The volcano was preparing to erupt. There was nothing one could say or do to console her, or selfishly myself.

How could this have happened? How could this be happening?

He was fifty-three years young and had barely scratched the surface of his life. He had so much more to live for and experience. What would our lives be like without him? He would not see his grandchildren or evidence of love he had so delicately manifested.

His death occurred at the beginning of the Remembrance Day long weekend, which meant a church funeral would be delayed until after the holiday Monday. The funeral was scheduled for November thirteenth, my Mother's forty-fifth birthday, a date she would never look forward to again.

When there was hard work to be done, one simply accepted the challenge and happily went about completing the task without excuses. Excuses were an alibi for weaknesses stemming from false fear. My father had the richest heart and consistently reached out always willing to help anyone who needed him. He understood giving was not about sharing. It was much more. It was the right thing to do. His qualities were stellar and he made everyone feel invited into his life. We were his students.

The arms of my mother and sister linked together as the Honor Guard saluted, signifying his arrival. The gesture was perfect.

On November twentieth, one week to the day of my father's funeral his mother died of a broken heart. My grandmother's heart was devoured by the loss of her oldest child. She followed to protect him and be with his soul.

While it was not justified by any means, there was a sense of relief; they crossed the bridge together. As always the details are in the suffering. Arriving home after the second funeral we were paralyzed with the reality of emptiness. Stung with shock and despair we quickly felt the void in our lives.

We were benefactors given love, joy and happiness from two beautiful people. It caused all of us to sit up and take notice of what each of us would take away from the knowing, loving, and grieving.

Human life begins here on earth, with intentions to survive creating legacies to be shared. No matter what you feel about your parents or grandparents they are the glue to survival. When my father was nine years old, he crossed the Atlantic with his mother from Poland to Canada. It was a long and dismal journey with little food and ill health yet there was a promise of hope in finding a better future. Seeking freedom from war and living in harmony was their ultimate goal. Woodbridge, Ontario became the first home for my grandparents and father.

My grandfather entered Canada one month earlier and did not find employment or housing for his anxious family on their way. The field of hope and dreams became their respite. It was a shanty house in an open field. Each day my grandmother begged for help believing in the kindness and compassion from strangers. One man came forward and offered to let them live in his home and provided safety from an otherwise desperate beginning.

On my twentieth birthday my father had finally answered some of the deep seeded and innocent questions forever lingering in my curiosity of those early years in Canada. When he finally found the strength to talk about their hardships endured my understanding of emptiness was cast in stone. Learning how poverty existed in my DNA enabled me to see all humans as poor. Instincts of survival enabled my family to flourish without need for pomp and circumstance. We lived in the village of our home with so much love and happiness. His flawless commitment to us was relentless. No matter what we ever said or did he found a way to make us feel accepted and always forgiven.

His death became another notch in the belt of greatest lives lost. He was the teacher of truth and servitude. Without his "Foreverness" the essence of life would never be understood. He inspired us to be creative, think out of the box and be inquisitive. He demanded we pray together and every Sunday we did. His appreciation for the silence in nature was never compromised.

We owned homes with magnificent rock gardens that he prided himself in creating for the benefit of others. His tapestry and canvas took on real terms of endearment. Our holiday trips were always planned around an unexpected treasure hunt. His appreciation for the earth demanded our attention at all times. We scoured the Black Hills, Mount Rushmore, corn fields in Iowa, forests in Algonquin Park always looking for and finding the beauty in the details.

◆◆◆

"You will share my good forever."

—St. Catherine of Genoa
Purgation and Purgatory, the Spiritual Dialogue

Nine

PEACE WITH GOD

On the twentieth anniversary of my Father's death a visit to his grave invited another moment with a heightened sense of impermanence.

The need to clean up the gravesite, before winter, was on the "to do" list for this particular beautiful Saturday afternoon. The sun was shining and the winds were brisk, but not chilling. As we drove around the graveyard my heart spoke "out loud." The words flew dangerously through my lips and even surprised me. "If my life ends today, there are no regrets as my life is complete." Those were the sentiments shared in the car as we parked at my Father's gravesite.

My hands were anxiously pulling the weeds seemingly anchored to the earth with more dedication than one had anticipated. Yanking, fighting and mentally urging them to leave the ground seemed inexplicably grueling. The task took a twist and within seconds there was a consistent stinging on my hands. Without warning a spiral of winged angels flew up from within the grave. They were yellow jacket wasps who had made a comfortable home in the garden below the headstone. As the nest was being unleashed the pheromones were activated. Within seconds the entire nest had been actively aggravated and resolved to leave their comfortable surroundings.

Running as fast as an Olympic sprinter the race began. My body was flung against the headstone as the realization, a swarming was taking place. Not having time to calculate their endurance or speed my feet jaunted across the graves with invisible Pegasus wings. Flying across the gravel with summer heels not only felt ridiculous but looked equally as crazy.

How would one ever discriminate between killing them to survive and loving them as they are beautiful sentient beings? My head was swimming with intensity of what to do next. My first gesture was to remove my sweater and cover my face. That is exactly what transpired. Blinded now by a lack of light and direction, my ears could only hear the voice of my husband screaming "run back to the car, the door is open."

Turning on a dime, waving the sweater above my head and covering my face in between, my feet ran well over five hundred feet on air. Within seconds, which felt like hours, my body thrust itself into the car and slammed the door shut. Gasping and taking long deep breathes, my heart was pounding and immediately the inside of the car became my sanctuary. However, in slow motion my eyes peered down upon my body as it became apparent several of the wasps had decided to partner with me during the jump. Without hesitation they were removed to the exterior of the car. We sped away as my body shook and the scene was replayed in my mind.

The first words that came out of my mouth…"What if there is an allergic reaction?" We quickly surmised that my body had acquired well over thirty stings on the neck, shoulders, and arms with the largest group of stingers in my fingers.

Without blinking, my husband said "You made peace with God minutes before we began the clean up! "Why do you care?" Stunned that he would make this his initial comment, yet it was true.

My knee-jerk reaction was to call the hospital. Just as these words were uttered…my body calmed down. The eloquent and always evident Wisdom Auditor arrived. The guest of an uninvited event yet always invited to be with commentary.

"Patricia, you have always been delicately aware of your impermanence, yet you have desired more life. Your mission is held with great interest. Mother Nature has spared your life. Do you understand why? This Divine wicked way of the world offers opportunities to be in the experience of the moment by being in between the moment. It is during this

time karma ripens. All that needs to be healed from the past is brought to us in the present and the result is set for the future when you choose."

Those who have felt the painful loss of a loved one, especially a parent, feel incredible loss inside the open heart. My wish to see and speak with my father again lives inside my mind every single moment. This never leaves me. He was an honorable man with great wisdom and integrity. It is because of him that my earthly moments have survived both trauma and question. Some of us have been given sensational, loving parents. It's not like that for everyone.

"For this reason you were spared death... You agreed to be mindful and live for even greater and more complex experiences, some of these will bring you great realizations. What is yet to come has the potential to unravel your ego, while challenging your patience but ultimately showing you the path."

In this fragile moment my heart knew the stingers were left behind as reminders of the suffering of those before me and would never be removed without remembering there are no excuses for the choices we make. Truth has no alibi.

Ten

WHEN LOVE FINDS YOU

What is transparent will be revealed only when the graphics of your dreams shake you until reality becomes the vision seen and not the vision that blinds you.

After the untimely death of my father, there was a tidal wave of bombastic pain. The suffering was relentless and the loss of being held so tightly in the beauty of love wore my heart thin and dehydrated like the skin of a cobra. The probability his life might have been extended if attention to his medical problems had been made a priority became brutally clear. Listening to his justifications and contemplations of denial brought frustration and concern. All one could do was remain the observer and believe he was smart enough to take better care of himself. Unfortunately, his choices were more of a sacrifice and made no sense to anyone but himself.

For years after his death my mother sank into the places where grief is less than kind as she held vigil for the man she met at the age of fifteen as a young hat check girl and he the dashing young hotel office manager, nine years her senior.

One could only imagine the poverty of the heart which followed after a war leaving people displaced and stranded. Homes were filled with strangers called "borders" who became instant family, and fridges were more empty than full. Her life was also somewhat weakened by the fact she had been diagnosed with a tumor in her leg and required surgical intervention. Her sister had died at the age of twenty- three months from a rare stomach disease which crippled the emotions of my grandparents. They became incredibly protective of their only living child. Life was filled with so many complexities in the 1930's and 1940's and left many people struggling for existence let alone the need for an operation.

My mother was left partially paralyzed after the tumor was removed. The doctor's prognosis was not favorable believing she may not walk for a very long time. There were no rehabilitation or therapy facilities available. The protocol was to keep the patient comfortable with the body and leg still, eliminate activities and stay in bed for several months to recover. She found courage which deepened her positive approach to recovery and began her own therapy. After missing so much school her options for the future were limited. She sought employment toward a productive career but with limited income potential. Sovereign Pottery was hiring and offered her a job. She accepted and within months an opportunity presented itself at the elegant downtown Sheraton Hotel. This was a gift of resolve as jobs were very scarce to begin with. Once again there was a destiny unraveling itself and without hesitation two soul mates were soon to find passion together.

As the flirtatious love between the handsome office manager and the hatcheck girl grew deeper the idea of marriage between them became a reality. They lived with my grandparents for one year. They insisted on a proper examination of behavior to assess their potential for a successful marriage. If they were found to be compatible, loving, and judged to be a good match, they would be free to wander the world together and that is almost exactly what happened.

After my father's passing, we found an old ledger in the attic with details of their monthly expenses and income from the year they lived with her parents. It was reviewed each month by my grandfather to ensure they were responsible and also saved a minimum of ten dollars per month. When the twelve month trial ended, they began the whirlwind life of relocating, birthing two children and finding happiness in the post-war world.

My father loved numbers and became a Certified General Accountant who passed the difficult examinations in New York with the highest marks. It was my dream to follow in his footsteps. My goal of becoming one of the first female Bank Managers was achieved at the age of twenty five. My father passed just days before this announcement.

For many years the tragedy of his death left my mother in a deep and very dark depression one she thought was hidden from us. She camouflaged her pain yet it surfaced often in her words. No one could blame her as life had taken her to a place of shared loneliness.

When grandchildren arrived she seemed to have found a rekindling of happiness and joy. Her suffering disappeared and her eyes danced with excitement as she nurtured her family now filled with children.

There are many aspects of family life which dominate the dynamics of our relationships. Some are built upon strengths and become the pillars of our future and others require examination. There will always be one story hidden yet demanding to be told. The gift of "noticing in the moment" has become the essence of my life and without hesitation the trigger soothed chaos into wisdom.

The Wisdom Auditor sensed my need for comfort and as we sat together at the edge of the bed he knew once more a miracle would be birthed. In the recipe for love the ingredients are spun into a fairy tale and sometimes they become the magical antidote for suffering. With an exhaustion only described as chemically induced my eyes closed and inside the ethers the visions lived.

We always felt my mother's routine was benign. She seemed confident and content and looked forward to evenings with her grandchildren, yet there was a mystery around her revealing painful remnants of a life without passion or love. It was a haunting visible through my heart.

Her vast knowledge of watches, batteries and details of the inner workings always amazed me as she brought her daily stories to life. She thought bookbinding repair was a great hobby and yet we never understood her passion as she disliked reading. What made her love the outside and exterior of a book so strongly she would volunteer at the school library to painstakingly repair them with such skill. It almost seemed she was afraid of the content inside. Could it be the stories would reveal the sorrows and losses she held deep in her psyche or was it the joy and gifts of love would be distant reminders of what she lived without?

The routine at work was as predictable as the routine at home. However, one typical day she greeted a gentleman at the counter who had need for jewelry repairs. She affirmed there was something "known" between them when their first words were spoken. He shared immediately he was a widower and lost his wife years earlier to cancer. She was taken by his soft and gentle demeanor yet she was visibly protective of her awareness towards him. His aliveness was made known to me during a routine daily phone call when she shared in a monotone voice how interesting this man was behaving as he brought one piece at a time to be re-plated every few days.

We begged for more information and were told, "Not your business". These were familiar words from the voice of one who chose quiet anonymity for much of her life.

She finally confessed to my sister she had been invited out for coffee by this very nice and kind gentleman.

This friend was now becoming a daily fixture at her coffee break time and the whispers in the store made her head swim with the dislike for gossip. She did not realize they actually reveled in her joy. She had reached out further than her handshake mentality. This was a shocking breakthrough for all of us as she actually sounded interested in him. The details of this Knight in shining armor were not handed over easily. The desire to know what he possessed that lured this woman who had lived for nearly twenty five years with one man and twenty-five years with no man became our obsession. We wanted to know him. She seemed quite calm and perhaps smitten with being sought after. She was not anxious to have dinner or invite him into her personal world of "us." Yet it was very clear the attention riveted her to work longer hours and with a subtle amnesia to the past.

She enjoyed the attention. We began to realize perhaps she might not be equipped with the skill to take this relationship further than the clinking of tea cups and niceties. Happiness became a new theme in her life and this wonderful breath of fresh air surrounding her was savored by all of us. Our curiosity could not be thwarted and relentlessly we asked posing questions yet she held her feelings tightly and asked us to be patient. We were living in a bubble of excitement for her as she walked around like an air-brushed photo each day as she left the house. He was a Knight in shining armor. There was no hesitation on our part to push her into this nirvana of the heart as we encouraged her to let us meet him.

Eleven

A VOICE IN HARMONY WITH THE UNIVERSE

The frost on the windows added a chill to this already damp and dreary March day. The work schedule for my mother had changed, and she was required to stay for an extended hour, which meant it would be dark as she took the bus home. There was no direct bus route causing her to wait in the bitter cold to transfer to a second bus. This would leave her at an intersection one block away from her home. In March the darkness set in earlier than six p.m. which meant the walk to her front door would be down a stark and naked street.

This was the home she demanded to live in again. In her mind, it was the safe place. She was raised here chalking the streets and playing with no knowledge of fear. After the untimely death of her mother she deeply missed being with her father. Our lives traversed residing in six cities in North America including Omaha, Nebraska for three years. She begged my father to consider a move closer so she could spend quality time with her father. This decision was easily made when they learned he had been diagnosed with pancreatic cancer and given less than two years to live. Time became precious for her and once again our family reinvented itself in a city and place. We moved into the home my mother was born in. The house was resurrected and updated by my father to meet the privacy necessary for five people to live comfortably.

After the death of her father and husband, we knew she would never be able to leave this red brick museum of her heart. The walls held her secrets and the ground held our only attachment to a past filled with the history of a family who found happiness and love beyond measure.

When the bus arrived downtown she neatly collected herself and sat for the twenty-two minute drive through the city, where she watched the familiar lights in the windows of houses and stores. She contemplated how close spring was and how she would enjoy the warmer temperatures.

She held no casual conversation and when her stop arrived, she pulled the bell and quietly exited the bus looking around at the four empty corners where only the street lights and her breath could be seen as she exhaled.

She carried her purse, her shoe bag and a plastic tote (a.k.a. poverty bag) with her lunch containers wrapped tightly around one arm as she swiftly crossed two sets of lights and began to walk past the alley and turn down the street towards her front door. What took place in a matter of twenty-two seconds rattled all of our lives forever. There is no ability to comprehend what Tiger Blood runs through the veins of those who have no mercy for life.

She recalled the sound of a train entering her ears. The pounding noise grew louder behind her and she quickened her step on the slippery wet sidewalk. She was less than fifteen feet away from her home when without warning three bodies jumped her and threw her to the ground. The screams from their voices she described as hyenas laughing and frothing. The smashing of a baseball bat across her head along with a continual slamming against her shoulder, arms and legs made the noise disappear. She was abandoned to a puddle of her own blood, where she lay unconscious.

What she refused to give up was the bundle of tightly wound bags in her possession, a poverty bag filled with emptiness. The three young culprits were only interested in finding money in her purse.

They were children without a conscience as they viciously attacked and fought to retrieve the poverty bag from her wrist. They managed to dislocate her shoulder, rip through her face and crushed her fingers until they were broken spindles.

The beating from the baseball bat to her face and body left bruises and scars as permanent reminders. As they kicked her into unconsciousness she remembered looking into their tiger eyes.

The street was quiet with very little walking traffic. It seemed impossible not one neighbor could hear her muffled screams or had window eyes to watch the sidewalk under the street light. The lifeless body of my mother, covered in her own blood drenched through the ripped and torn coat. She fell into the perishable time zone as she had no concept of being alive. Would she be found before she succumbed to her injuries? An hour had passed and no one walked down the street until a young neighbor, who was returning home from her evening school classes, realized with disbelief she was looking at my mother's body. She knew her well and was terrified to touch her and see if she was alive or dead. She ran home without breathing and quickly dialed my sister's phone number and 911. Within minutes an ambulance arrived and transported her to the hospital.

Having just returned from a short vacation, a phone call from my mother and sister was normally expected. We are very close and checking in with one another was routine. This phone call however was trapped in someone else's voice.

There was no "hello" or calmness on the other end of the line. The sounds grunted were distinctly crafted yelps of words like Mom, attack, blood, and hospital now!

Those feeble attempts to create comprehensive words finally came together and my body sank onto the floor in shock. Moments later my feet sprinted to the car. Upon arrival to the emergency department, we were greeted by the nursing staff, who cautiously guided us to her bed.

The doctors made her comfortable although she had a very difficult time staying awake. Nothing could have prepared me for the moment we were eye to eye. The step back into the non-existent wall to hold me up was quickly halted by the invisible hand of Wisdom Auditor. The grim reality set in as the body in front of me had been marginalized by a brutal assault. Not the blood or swelling of her face and ripped eye shocked me as much as the thought of her being terrorized by the hyenas without a conscience.

The following week my father-in-law, who had been suffering with dementia, passed away and the anguish of burying one parent in the dirt of the earth and aid in healing of another from the dirt of a sidewalk awakened the spirit of impermanence.

The sidewalk fostered good memories from her childhood. Now it had lied to her, just like Aida had lied to me. The trappings of place where people have no regard for one another added another wound. Bricks and mortar were not emotional; they were forms which held ritual and darkness when the light failed to expose them.

How does one begin to think about creating positive feelings after such trauma? How would one trust any human being from this day forward? My heart wanted to remove these memories from both her and my mind. It was my call to duty. The moment we are taken to the doorway of someone's insanity we are in relationship. We may not have been politely introduced or know why we meet however it has been designed.

My helpless mother held onto her belongings unaware by doing so, she had given them permission to attack. If she had thrown her bag down, they might have spared her this brutal beating.

Despite her heroic effort the thieves managed to remove her purse from her unconscious body.

What resulted from the take was equivalent to a slot machine win of less than seventeen dollars. The police scoured the streets looking for witnesses, and drove up and down hoping to find a clue or trace of her purse. Not long after her release from the hospital, there was a visit by the Detective who had been assigned to her case. Her purse had been found, three blocks away in a backyard. Her wallet was emptied of money and her identification left intact. It was as if they knew better. For some strange reason my mother recalled that one of the participants in her assault was a female. The revelation sparked a great interest in the case as there had been five similar incidents in the city over several months prior to her attack. What was not known before was the gender of all the assailants. They were not just male.

The voices of the boys were deep and angry and the girl who knew violence in her Monkey Blood spoke with calmness and a familiarity.

This was not the first time they had done this. It was obvious to my mother they knew all too well what they were doing.

This new information made great sense to the Detective as he declared the makeup bag in her purse had been emptied. Obviously the young female took her share of the trophy. We knew she would look like a clown wearing someone else's costume.

The days following left everyone anxious and fearful. It was extremely difficult for my family to look into the eyes of every neighbor wondering with distinct curiosity if they were all hiding behind their window curtains watching innocently with guilty pleasure. How could this scene from a movie take place without someone coming forward?

Unable to walk upstairs to her bedroom a makeshift respite was created in the living room. Those first few days we worked very carefully and cautiously to ensure she knew how loved and cared for she would be. The road to her recovery was difficult and her physiotherapy required not only a positive attitude by her, but a willingness to walk out the front door on each occasion. This, all by itself, became a prison sentence. There was no way to console the woman who chose to live in her safe haven knowing someone, somewhere, somehow knew where she lived and had already marked their territory. We worked relentlessly to comfort her and ensure she knew the safety net was always there.

There would always be one reminder that would never go away. It took more than a year to eliminate the blood stains tattooed on the cement sidewalk in front of the house. She stared at its blank face every day as she fought back tears and languished over what her future would be like.

It was a haunting reminder for all of us. We bleached, painted and washed the sidewalk regularly knowing it had its own memory. The screams will always stain the walkway when it greets us.

The awakenings in between each breath constantly reminded her of the nightmare. While this was one hand of life sculpting a theatre of the macabre there was another waiting for the woman who no longer showed up to share her time and tea.

There was a man who sat and waited patiently every day hoping his friend would arrive to spend her fifteen minute break with him.

After a few weeks of her absence, he decided to do a little personal investigation and marched into the store seeking out the manager for questioning.

He had become the gentle and all too familiar customer with more than a quest for a repaired piece of antiquity. He asked not about the date for the return of his silver, but rather he asked if the Golden Goddess of the repair department no longer worked there.

The room fell silent as everyone realized he did not know what had happened to his Goddess. With her head hung low, the manager gazed up and smiled at the Knight who came looking for his Princess. He was quietly informed she would not be coming back. It was as devastating for her to tell him as it was for him to receive this news. He stood gallantly as he fought back his tears and tried to imagine what insane and evil persons could bring harm to her.

Permission had been given ahead of time should he ever come looking for her it would be acceptable to give him her phone number. As the manager handed over the piece of paper they both felt the uncomfortable intensity of loss. Everyone watched him leave the store as he was visibly shaken and without doubt now on a mission.

Immediately upon arriving home the phone call was made and one visit together was all it took. There is no explanation for what the heart is capable of doing when the echoes of past lives resurface.

It never even occurred to us her vulnerable life would ever find complete contentment again. The source of happiness came from tragedy as the lotus is birthed from the mud.

People do believe in angelic intervention. Based on the cycle of all things sacred, this was evidence in magical proportion. It was clearly beyond imagination. Within eight days after his initial visit she moved her entire life to join with her Knight who met her holding the silver anvil.

He literally carried her from the threshold she had walked through most of her life, ensuring her feet did not touch the Tiger Blood on the sidewalk. This was the blood now shattering her trust in humanity. He became her constant companion and caregiver. She moved into the place where the four walls held the secrets of his life, yet he was willing to share his dreams and open the expanse of his heart to her.

One cannot know the depth of emotion unless you risk meeting its challenge. It was now a love affair. They were two lovely people gifted with time. They were inseparable beings drawn together by the magnet of trauma.

Meeting him for the first time, my eyes were like those of a cat, analyzing every aspect of him. What he did took my breath away. He was the essence of humility and compassion and within seconds he was fully known to me. The years evaporated into powdered milk. He had a willingness to share with a kindness that was so rare.

His fragile life had also felt the pangs of loss and he too was looking for the sunshine that appears after the rainbow, not the rainbow after the rain.

The dirt rose under the sidewalk of life and blossomed into the most beautiful lotus and the scent of Forget-me-nots lingered in the room. He had not only fallen in love with my mother, he was reincarnated love to all of us. The story became one so unlikely simply put, it was a fairytale.

The moment of 'knowing' had taken place and the bond had long existed. We were a family again and the importance of how it happened or the need to focus on the circumstances would only serve to reduce its perfection.

The cessation of her suffering evaporated. They spent days and days together sharing their life stories over a tea pot that never emptied. Gradually, she recovered with obvious intermittent pain and extreme difficulty in raising her arm above the shoulder. We believed things were very fine and did not expect what came up next.

Maybe it was guilt? Whatever triggered her phone call to my sister to come and get her upset all of us. She wanted to come home.

When we sat with her, we realized she had made an incredible physical recovery however had not yet fully dealt with her emotional trauma and confusion had entered.

He had clarity and said he would be patient. For five days she cried and cried and never left the house or her chair. The trauma overcame her and caused us much concern as we all felt her sadness and fear. We were helpless in bringing justice or redemption to the table.

We kept the man who appeared as her Knight up to date. On the sixth day he arrived and carried her away for the second time across the threshold with her feet never touching the cement sidewalk still covered in the Monkey Blood. From that moment on, they inhaled life together.

If this tragedy had not happened, we believe she would be sitting at every tea break smiling at her lovely friend never experiencing more than a two minute flirtation just like the boiled water awaits the tea bag to flourish. Their lives changed by the hand and gift of love, so did ours.

We celebrated by sharing holidays and trips to his summer trailer up north.

The birds seemed to migrate away from all other units to be in concert with them alone. One could never imagine how serendipity became the nuance of such a treasure amidst so many painful memories. It was wonderful to be part of their growing love and every day another page of joy was written into their storybook.

My personal "forever to remember moment" with our Knight was during a visit up north. One spectacular summer's night after the sun had set and the light of the moon danced across the calm waters. We sat in the car and listened to Stairway to Heaven.

In that space of time, we imagined a chorus of angels had blessed our lives sanctifying forgiveness was not only the necessary emotion to happiness but we learned the secret to its equation; self-love.

It was important we prayed for those who wronged as they needed our compassion as well as forgiveness. It did not matter if they knew this or not during this lifetime. We had learned the essence and truth. We would not forget. Instead the moments were replaced with "Foreverness."

There was an appreciation for all things perfect as they aligned that evening. When the music finished the echo lingered and neither of us wished to break silence. For me, it was another moment of recognizing impermanence. It was similar to the night when my love handed me the card with the silhouette of a young girl with cascading tears. Was it a sign of an unwelcomed tomorrow? When the car engine was turned off the silence was numbing, and we jumped out, walking side by side, content we had found the space to heal my mother.

November was a cold month and on the evening of my husband's birthday we celebrated as a family. A conversation began and there was a stabbing in my heart with an invisible dagger. Our Knight shared prostate cancer had been detected. This news, while not well received by any of us, felt like the sinking of the Aida. He had become my Guardian Angel and everyone else's.

All things happening in and out of my world were held in his trust. He did not judge me. He did not ridicule me, he simply allowed me to trust in him. He opened the channel to his heart wide enough the universe could fit all of us in it. He was the eye of the needle and my red string of life fit through it and looped back to always find his hand holding the other end.

The years following were filled with a continuum of joy and memories. When the disease ravaged and began to eat away at his body, my mother became his Angel of Life.

The man who unconditionally bestowed her with hope and nurtured her through an epic Dark Night of the Soul received a gift of perfect love. The opportunity to reciprocate now presented itself.. During the weeks of his failing the living room became a hospice. My mother devoted herself flawlessly to his care. Never leaving his side she had finally been given a chance to prepare without shock.

Not once other than for radiation and chemotherapy was he ever left alone. My sister and her daughters held vigil daily as payment for dues not only owed from the past, but also coins in the fountain of wishes for finding each other in the future.

Courage was missing the afternoon of my last visit with him. My hands held his ever so gently and into his ears "I love you" was whispered.

It is hard to fathom you can meet a person who has reached the state of Grace dignified to walk amongst the liars and thieves and still make you believe in dreams. This was a karmic alibi.

He was a man of grace and elegance, not cut from the average cloth, but rather a royal robe. My two loves had already met and joined their hearts and now the Halleluiahs would begin again.

The decision to leave before his moment of passing was one of the most difficult. His death was imminent. He loved me as his daughter and our bond was never to be broken. He along with my father lived life well exuding kindness and compassion.

It was my mother's hand that closed his eyes as he took his very last breath. How fitting they could be there for one another, unscripted and without doubt supported by the army of crimson angels hovering over their lives. My mother had once before been in the presence of this kind of love and death.

It reminded me of the Aria "Bist du bei mir" found in the notebook of Anna Magdelena Bach written for her husband Johann Sebastian Bach.

"When thou art near,
I go with joy
To death and to my rest.
O how pleasant would my end be,
If your fair hands
Would close my faithful eyes."

Shortly after six-thirty p.m. the house phone rang and it was my mother, NOW the messenger, who shared he was lifted to heaven. Tears burst forth and without warning my sobbing began. At first my head was clear and content to just relax into the knowing that heaven had erupted to open the gates for his arrival and for sure there were two souls waiting to put their angel wings around him. When the expansive heart feels itself fully there is only emotion running madly through it and there is no way of stopping the rainbow of sparkling tears. It was a completion as we had both reached the perfect state of realization.

What took place next seemed too surreal to imagine and was clearly a message from a place beyond this one. Sitting at my desk trying to compose myself my cell phone started to ring.

The ring was not pre-programmed. This was a shrieking mixture of Dixieland jazz and whistling. In total disbelief the screen prompted a line reading ZERO ZERO ZERO ZERO ZERO ZERO. It made no sense at all and my immediate thought was this must be the sleep alarm which had never been set. The music continued becoming louder and louder without relief. Another thought arrived as the air seemed so aromatic, somehow we had tapped into the sense of humor of the Universe. Bursting into laughter my voice yelped a very big "thank you and I love you!" It was the Knight saying good-bye kissing the airwaves with his magical presence. Whether this moment was a co-incidence set up by the cellular network out of control in the airwaves, or it was truly a miracle of communication from beyond, it did not matter.

The joy was spectacular and it was the latter which became my believable choice. Nothing will ever change my mind.

During the week of his demise my sister needed to attend a family member wedding in California. She was fraught with hesitation whether to stay home to be with our Knight and my mother or leave. Her bond with the Knight ran deep. Everyone convinced her she should celebrate life and be with her extended family. He would not be alone. With great sorrow she visited him and said her goodbye. She sheltered her tears from him and we all felt the struggle of her decision. The outcome would not change. She too was his daughter.

The wedding ceremony took place in a lovely historic church with vows created by the Bride and Groom. How ironic they had chosen this very day to proclaim their love, the same day the Divine took our special one from us.

When the words "I do" were spoken the stain glass windows exploded with a brilliant spectacle of light causing everyone to sit up and take notice. The dinner celebration was incredibly elegant, yet everyone was aware the Universe was calling our Knight to his rank and file above.

As the speeches began the Minister asked for a moment of silence and reflection. A special prayer and blessing was being offered to acknowledge the life now passing. Everyone bowed their heads and my sister looked down at her purse as it was vibrating. It was her cell phone. The phone number was from his home. It was my mother leaving the message that he had just passed away, precisely during the prayer for his life.

The following morning my sister took a walk with her friend. They arrived at the longest pier built in San Diego. She recalled the quietude and sheer bliss of seeing nature in fullness and began to feel the sadness of returning home to emptiness. They were completely alone.

This was an oddity as the peer was a tourist attraction and a very busy place. A phone was ringing and they realized it was coming from her purse. The screen was lit with "ZERO ZERO ZERO ZERO, ZERO" and when she answered there was no voice on the line.

They proceeded to walk further down the peer and could hear a phone ringing again, this time it was ahead of them in an emergency phone box. They looked at one another laughing and said "Who is phoning us out here?"

The water was loud and the waves were crashing up against the peer and the volume of the phone became louder and louder. Picking up the receiver there was no one at the other end.

The irony was later shared by my sister. She made a declaration out loud it was our Knight making sure she knew he was okay. What she did not know was he too had called me.

Upon return from the wedding, she recited the phone stories to my mother who stared blankly into her face. Numb with surprise to hear the story she had already heard from me. My mother had not shared my experience with anyone. When she told my sister we each received the same call we hit pay dirt.

During our next visit together we showed one another our phone messages. It was a show and tell of the "Zero Zero Zero's." We smiled and knew there were no words of logic or denial. We had found "Foreverness".

He had shown us how to be in awe of each person, as we are magnificent and flawless creations. Even if you cannot understand one's motivation, you should never judge.

Our lives had been made richer for knowing such a fine gentleman, like my father who held mankind with the highest of regard. Yes, we knew we were very lucky.

My mother returned to the sidewalk once covered with Monkey Blood. This time, she danced to the music of her own choice and with confidence she crossed over the path with her feet fearlessly touching the cement. Finding peace had been a very long and arduous journey for her. Her life was made complete as she found the courage to step into the place where love once began and returned. This was another perfect karmic alibi.

◆◆◆

"Fletcher Lynd Seagull, do you want to fly so much that you will forgive the Flock, and learn, and go back to them one day and work to help them know?"

—Jonathan Livingston Seagull, Richard Bach

Twelve

THREE GIFTS TO THE PATH

Looking for the quaintest, most beautiful location in France became a bucket list item. Every weekend in one of the local newspapers there were various advertisements for dreamy villas with perfect sunset views. There was one repeatedly flirting with us. So smitten by the ad it was faithfully cut out and placed in the "if maybe possible" file. The name alone offered a sense of endearment. It was called The Sunflower apartment. Each weekend our curiosity grew and finally the call was made.

The owner was extremely excited about the property and invited me to drop by his home to view the photographs and discuss the location and its proximity to other places of interest.

The walk through his front door became the gateway towards another gift. After looking at the images and the serene paysage it became very clear this was a serendipitous location. Without blinking an eye, an on the spot decision was made and the Sunflower Apartment would become our home away from home for the bucket list holiday. An invitation to take a stroll through the art collection of the owner's home was extended. My eye fixated on an abstract painting of a beautiful white horse. The painting was named "Atila."

Curiosity generated a glance at the bottom of the canvas to view the name of the artist. It was noted the artist had a Serbian name. A conversation pursued and the owner of the painting said "ah no... The gentleman artist is French!" Clearly this might become a point of contention. The history of the gentleman artist was very interesting. Born in the former Yugoslavia, he chose France as his home in order to thrive and experience his passion for art. Learning he lived in the south of France my intention and desire to meet him was now deepening.

There was something powerful drawing me to his energy. The request was made, "might you assist in making an introduction?" His response was very clear. "He is quite eccentric, lives in a little village on the opposite side of Mt. Ventoux and one cannot predict his willingness to meet." Oh goodness, this was not an obstacle! The possibility of making his acquaintance now became the greater reason for the trip. We were off to France.

After a few days of blissfully celebrating the most glorious place on earth, the urgent request to meet the gentleman artist was made known to him. He reluctantly agreed to a three hour visit at his atelier (studio). We were given very specific directions and instructions on finding the village, informed that it was a bit of a tricky journey. The appointment was scheduled for two p.m. on Friday.

The directions were reasonably straight forward if you knew the highway and inner routes. The journey to the village would take close to four hours. Friday arrived and we headed out around ten a.m. with a sense the day would be very special. The drive was beyond anything one could imagine. At every corner, every round about and every village we inhaled the beauty, isolation and culture. It was intoxicating. Around one p.m. we arrived at the base of the mountain. We were on target to be on time.

The road signs were somewhat confusing. The posted destination offered two alternative routes. The decision was innocently made and we followed the wrong one. Two hours had passed and there were no signs indicating we were anywhere close. Driving through the mountain on slender tires, narrow passages and steep winding turns my tolerance began to thin and anxiousness prevailed.

It was now four p.m. as we arrived at the gates of the tiny village. My heart was beating faster than a race horse.

Would the Gentleman Artist understand? We quickly parked in the public lot behind the church and immediately saw the Gentleman

Artist sitting on the grand white rock outside of the only bakery in the village. Without question his response to our lateness was halted when our apologies were viewed as obviously innocent. We were visibly more upset than he was. He seemed disinterested with our tardiness yet somehow intrigued with our effort to make such a long drive to meet him.

In silence we walked to the ancient fortress he called home. Somehow the blemish of our lateness quickly subsided. We engaged in conversation sitting by the hearth inside the living room just outside the turret leading to his atelier. During the examination a subtle comment was made about birth places. By virtue of one degree of separation both he and my husband lived less than fifty kilometers from one another at birth. A bond had been forged. There is no synchronicity in life, only the recognition of it while on the path. He invited us upstairs to the atelier where he worked daily. It was beyond what one could envision. We spent the following two hours inhaling his stories and learning more and more about his very simple yet highly brilliant life. It was a rare glimpse into the fascinating world of a genius. He was gracious and generous to accommodate our insistent drop in, but the visit was now coming to an end.

The evening air was calm and the sky was filled with the most brilliant light from the full moon. The silence was meaningful.

Finally, the Gentleman Artist spoke and asked me three questions. Are you in this for the money? Do you want to be famous? Do you want to follow a path that might rip away your ego and find wisdom?

He extended his hand and invited me to return the following October to spend one week with him in the atelier. The invitation was gratefully and humbly accepted. Time could not move fast enough. Finally the week arrived and turned into an amazing and flawless friendship now lasting nearly over a decade and a half.

A voice whispered it was the Wisdom Auditor, *"My dear Patricia, what do you take away from this experience? Did you ever expect to meet the artist who will be chosen as one of the greatest geniuses of the future? What are your feelings now, after he agreed to spend more than a decade with you?*

Oh! Wisdom Auditor, in order to find the sage within, humility was needed. My heart was awakened to the creative echo of spirit within. There are principles grounded in deep tradition. All required of me was to be fully present, open to listening and a willingness to try. The wonderment of spending time in the sacred and precious atelier stirred far more than successful paintings. All mysteries of life were examined. He is a brilliant Master of patience, compassion and kindness.

A decade later an invitation to exhibit with him in France was accepted. My life felt complete.

The creative spark multiplies over time, after releasing all you thought you knew.

"Patricia, where did he take you?" He took me to the path where the recognition of self was mirrored in the work and the oneness birthed again.

◆◆◆

High up in the Himalayan mountains are many monasteries and retreats. Many of these are destinations for truth seekers whether they are in a formal or informal practice. There are also those who have made a commitment to the oneness of mankind. Searching for the meaning of life and the true nature of mind became a calling at a very early age for Ani Ngawang Pema, a Sherpa Buddhist nun.

Her story is special to me because she is related to one of my dearest friends. This knowledge however was not made known to me until her death.

A National Geographic documentary had surfaced with Wade Davis a photographer and explorer and Matthieu Ricard a monk who is declared to be the happiest man in the world. They had successfully been granted a brief visit with Ani and the moment was captured on film.

Ani studied in Tibet from the age of twelve until she was twenty. She moved back to Nepal and lived in solitary retreat (meditation) for the better part of sixty years praying for all sentient beings of the six realms of Samsara. She had devoted her entire life to practicing the Dharma. Just knowing about her and the dedication to living in this holy and pure state of being was enough to drive me to further my studies in the esoteric and tantric teachings. She became my inspiration and instrument of my heart.

During a conversation with my lovely friend Nima who is a Sherpa from the Khumbu Valley in Nepal it was revealed that Ani indeed was part of her family.

Nima gave me the sad news that Ani had been ill and passed away on November 20th, 2010. A part of me wept with such sadness as she was an anchor for goodness in the world. Her repetitive mantra and prayers weakened the evil of the world. With her physically gone it felt like a gap in the vibration of prayer would be felt. Somehow our karmic connection had been revealed. After seeing her face for less than ten minutes during the documentary she had made an impact on my life and practice. For months my head thought only about abandoning all things in my world. The desire to visit her retreat home was added to the "if maybe someday" list. Her life was auspicious as she was a Dakini in human form dedicated to serving all sentient beings.

What a blessing to have known she had lived during the same days as me and we breathed the same air during our life time. Ani was given a very important burial. No one was allowed to touch her body for seven days.

One of the cousins left Canada to visit Nepal. He was informed the monks had given the family a few of the beads (thanga) from the mala/rosary that Ani wore every day. It was proposed one of the thanga beads would be given to my friend Nima. This was shared with me the morning the bead was placed around my neck.

Patricia my little force....You chose to be part of the cycle of transformation by choice. The circle of life is part of your heart and required to be connected with Ani in this lifetime. Your connection to her is a reflection of the work necessary for all of humanity. It is said one is able to choose their moment of release of consciousness.

Ani had practiced "Thugdam" as she had the power to give up her life at will. Many have been blessed by her as she demonstrated the highest state of being. Your journey has now been blessed beyond measure. You do not have to feel special or worthy. You simply have taken the baton in the other hand. For the race is always taking place. There is no finish line. If you think you have crossed it, you will only find yourself at the beginning of another.

◆◆◆

The unexpected call from Cambodia arrived and as my head was listening to the voice at the other end there was a grand moment of a "knowing." My dear friend had taken a trip to Thailand and found herself in the beautiful sacred grounds of Angkor Wat and the jungle surrounding it. She met a young man who was out of robes. He appeared to be very hip and almost rock star like. She struck up a conversation and learned he in fact was living on the grounds in a small orphanage which was run by the nuns and monks. He had been a victim of the Khmer Rouge and lived for nearly eighteen years alone in the jungle with other children. His story was nearly too difficult to digest. He shared more examples of his life and how one monk by the name of Master Keo Ann selflessly took the children into the Pagoda and gave them food, clothing and a place to stay. The conditions she described as most unfavorable.

However, there was something happening at the entrance to the grounds that made her jaw drop. The footings for a new building were being laid. She asked, what is the purpose of this building? With a brilliant smile the young man said "we are building a library"!

The Khmer regime had destroyed not only its people but its history and folklore. Fortunately the monks were able to salvage some of the written teachings by burying them in the stupas. Years have passed and the country is now stable and rebuilding itself. The monks have begun to rewrite the stories for future generations. The only words she uttered were "this has your name all over it" and hung up. Fast forward "it did."

She connected me with the young man and additional information was received regarding the needs required to finish the library. It was clear this was my calling. Master Keo Ann shared his commitment to assisting the Cambodian people in whatever way he could. He was caring for nearly 40 children on a daily basis. He provided them with daily teachings in a make shift school and some of the younger children were allowed to live in a make shift house. The library was to become part of the new history of Cambodia. My mind was no longer ruled by thinking, it was ruled by my heart.

Without hesitation my commitment was made and the library was built. In 2007, my first journey was made to visit China and Cambodia.

As my feet hit the soil there was no doubt my decision to help was profound. This was going to be a lifelong love affair with Cambodia. The library was a magnificent structure complimenting the Khmer architecture with exquisite attention to detail. As the door opened and the books on the shelf were shown to me, tears flowed down both my cheeks. Many books were covered in plastic and each one was well loved.

The journey back to Canada was filled with new ideas as if a refresh button had been hit. After letting things settle in my mind, the decision to look at the future with them took place. An inquiry into the possibilities of building a sustainable pagoda with real living quarters and facilities was put forward. By 2011 we had built showers, washrooms and an operational kitchen area.

A phone call arrived from my contact person who advised Master Keo Ann would like to build a school for the monks. He would like to host the first Prayer Day and reunion for the monks and children since the genocide. Garments, food and robes would be required. In addition a proper school with desks and chairs were needed. This was accomplished and the results were overwhelming.

Hundreds of monks, nuns and children from the region arrived to pray for three full days of ceremony and teachings. Millions of tears were shed for the departed and prayers were offered for the living in memory of the souls who suffered for their country and allegiance to humanity.

My visit in 2013 solidified the sustainability and confirmed my belief in "foreverness." We are one race.

Thirteen

LAST CALL

The Wisdom Auditor watched as my body washed up on the banks of the Euphrates. The Wisdom Auditor watched as the eclipse shifted the light upon my coffin.

The Wisdom Auditor sat on the peak of Kailash as my boots were swishing their way up to the summit. It was there that my voice was finally heard. The seven peaks of blue snow were crisp and foreign to my breath, but welcomed without hesitation.

We looked at photos in picture frames together. Faces were no longer blurred but were in full view with streams of light from behind their pixel form. Wonderful images made me choke as visions streamed passed and the reason to "BE" became known.

Life jolted many electrons through the layers of my skull. Words permeated and hands were thrust through the evidence of all things future. What now transpired was the joy of being content to know everyone and every moment lives on in "Foreverness."

Hand-in-hand we vanished into the ethers.

Fourteen

PATRICIA'S WORDS

Every now and then there is a longing to melt words together. The great poets Shakespeare, Goethe, Hafiz and Rumi all wrote to shake us up emotionally and create appreciative inquiries into what creates inspiration for change and motivation. Sometimes it evokes a temperament of challenge and we look fear straight in the eyes.

As accomplished as many of these poets were in Literature, Mathematics, Medicine, Physics and Religion they aspired to offer words from a deep source within. These sages devoted their lives to revealing wisdom in a variety of patterns. Most often their words ignited us into a re-think or a moment of genuine contentment. When I was thirteen there was a great desire to learn from the Psalms and King David's perfect revelations.

Over time many attempts were made to articulate life from this poetic perspective. This culminated in a deluge of poetic liberties. Many were left on the cutting room floor. Yet there was a moment of triumph and balance achieved. Based on a few of the stories shared in Karmic Alibi, I have chosen four pieces penned over the past decades. In hindsight, writing poetry was not a means of therapy, rather a belief in the idea thoughts turned into words could make a difference. To share them reveals a memory tied into part of the dream we awaken to when they are read. I hope you will find meaning in the words.

◆◆◆

LIFE

Distant valleys, slow moving streams, deep within my heart
Washing away my awakening dreams, until death arrives to part
Love birds cooing, men stewing, as nature instils her fear
As puzzles of rivers christen the moments,
With a silence of violent cheer
Puddles thriving like fast flowing streams,
Swiftly ushering thoughts through the air
Splashing into the emptiness, crushing away all fear
Animals hunting, men hoping, as existence politely shares
Here is the beginning we have waited for
As every breathe becomes aware
Moistened drops will end the sorrow, predestined by our hearts
And ignorance will coerce all time to flee from lying passionate starts
And channel intentions until rebirth virtually stops.

◆◆◆

ATTIC OF MY MIND

Rummaging through the attic of my mind
I found a little something
Menacing an impartial corner it was a façade of a memory left
Aimlessly lost unto itself
Yet visible to only its aggressor
A poison portrait boldly stared with a daggering shard of light
Dancing off the royal windows into the jealous night
Simple me laughing, as the sound revealed the shame
Of one stale dream caught in the clouds
Like a senseless quivering flame

No logic framed this dismal curse
Or gave reason to commit
His love would die a remorseful death
An uninvited victim in her universe
Remove the hate and leave the room she joyfully declared
For all is lost and nothing more can ever here be spared.

There is no hope for an appeal as the illusion calls your name
You my friend are lost in time amidst the mirror of one so vain
Forbid the cobwebs from hovering in the womb of your dream
As they revel in your lusty pain
Rest quietly now and starve not
As this mirage is not to blame,
Let it rummage through and rest awhile
For it found you in the mundane,

In the attic of your mind.

◆◆◆

SPIRIT FLOWERS

What is my update?
Why did I decide to tell you?
I don't know what the truth is
They only schedule me…
My cancer is radical
My feelings are maniacal
The days are so managed as I walk into their shoes
Slightly tapping behind their news
Slightly listening to their pitiful blues

My cancer is now a drug
Warped in and out of love
It's just a word for them to use
As I saddle into their trust
As I become their muse

My little slippers use to fit my feet
But they took them away from me
They gave me slip on sheets and said
Like this a lot, cause it's really cheap
And I said "why bother with me""
Did you not really see?

I am torn between the ethers
My own death sentence meandering
Capturing all their glances
In a fractured philandering
Filled with remorse for the moments behind
With a future construct leaving hope aligned

I am fifth in the ethers
Not designed for this date
I am lost in the garden
Knowing I'm late…

Who will hand me
My spirit flowers?

◆◆◆

THE FINAL CHAPTER ONE

It always begins with the same moan
The centre of the belly spilling out dark loam
Like a cloud of air it gathers speed
And without any logic dances into the greed
The final Chapter one is always the same
As the pain never ceases nor shares in the blame

The never ending silence spins a vacuum in space
Where the impact is honorable not marred by disgrace
The same words
The same lines
Feelings never change
The life that once lifted,
Now weighed down in chains

For the sake of the final Chapter one
And all time it takes to create

The victory is already destined by its dancing fate
In the womb of thought the score is smudged
As they await the karmic judge

Bloody lady cries in the night
Scorching the blackened sky
She hides herself amidst the stars
Waiting for her victims with delight
Tear drops sting her tongue
While waiting for the final Chapter one.

Fifteen

Mastering THE FIVE RADICAL DEGREES OF LIFE

Degree One: RISK
Degree Two: ROOT
Degree Three: REMEDY
Degree Four: REALIZATION
Degree Five: REALITY

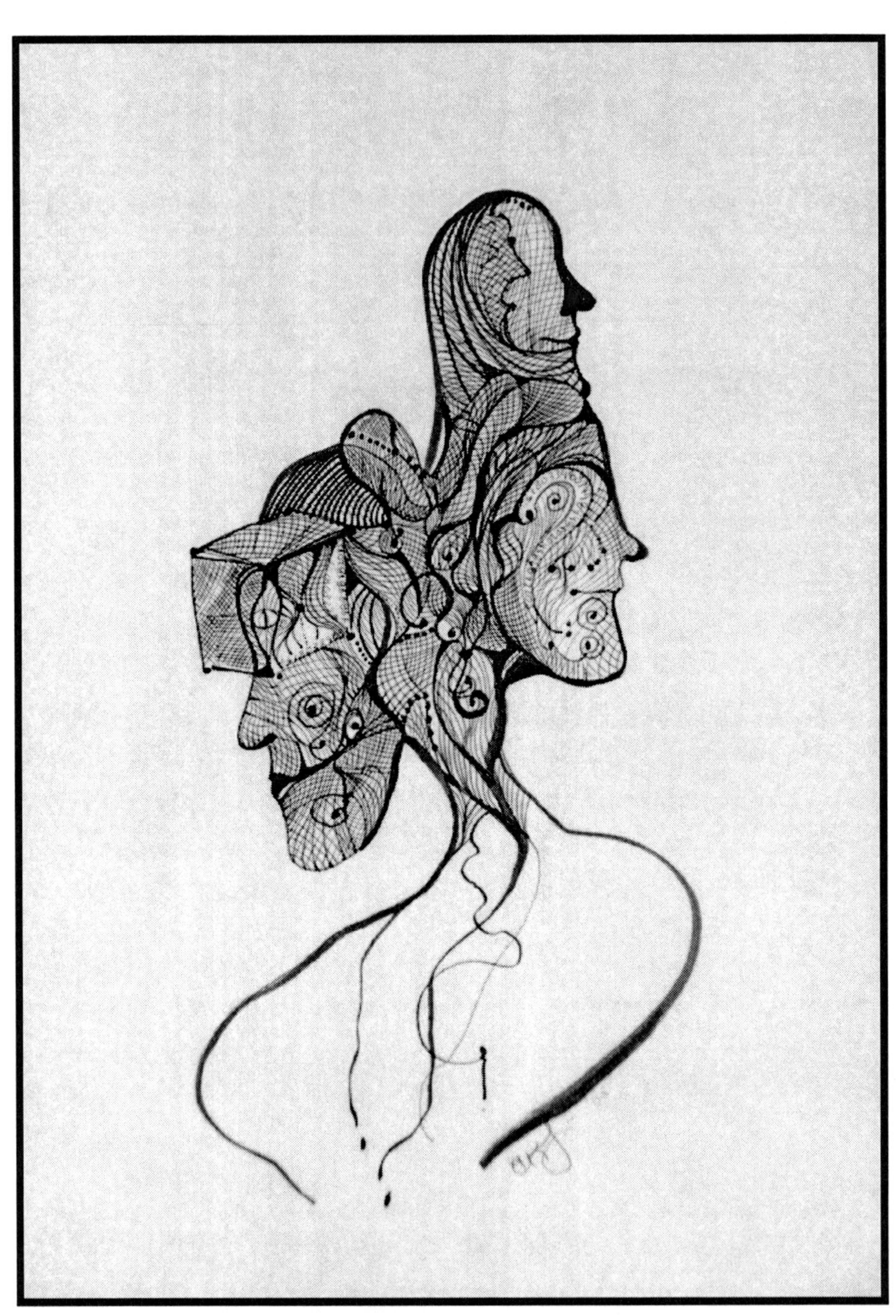

(Illustration created by Author.)

DEGREE ONE: RISK

Imagine a world without risk. Would you follow the unexpected path leading to the unknown? Habitually, we stay safe but in unpredictable moments when we risk it all, the hand of fate, destiny or karma arrives. Risk is an illusion we create for ourselves. When our motivations are out of the ordinary our lives become more meaningful and beneficial for others. In truth, there is no risk. When we practice external relaxation and internally do the work paying extra-ordinary attention to our attitude we generate deep compassion and experience a powerful purification.

Inspired to be Rewired triggers a creative impulse and inspiration; guiding your inner wisdom to manage with patience the Radical Risk inside you. The work to be accomplished by all human beings is to be found in the happiness of this life. Seek to train the mind with contemplations and meditations resulting in making wiser and better choices. Learn to value the risk involved with a measurement that is shaped by you alone. As you begin living a happier more phenomenal existence, everyone profits, not just yourself.

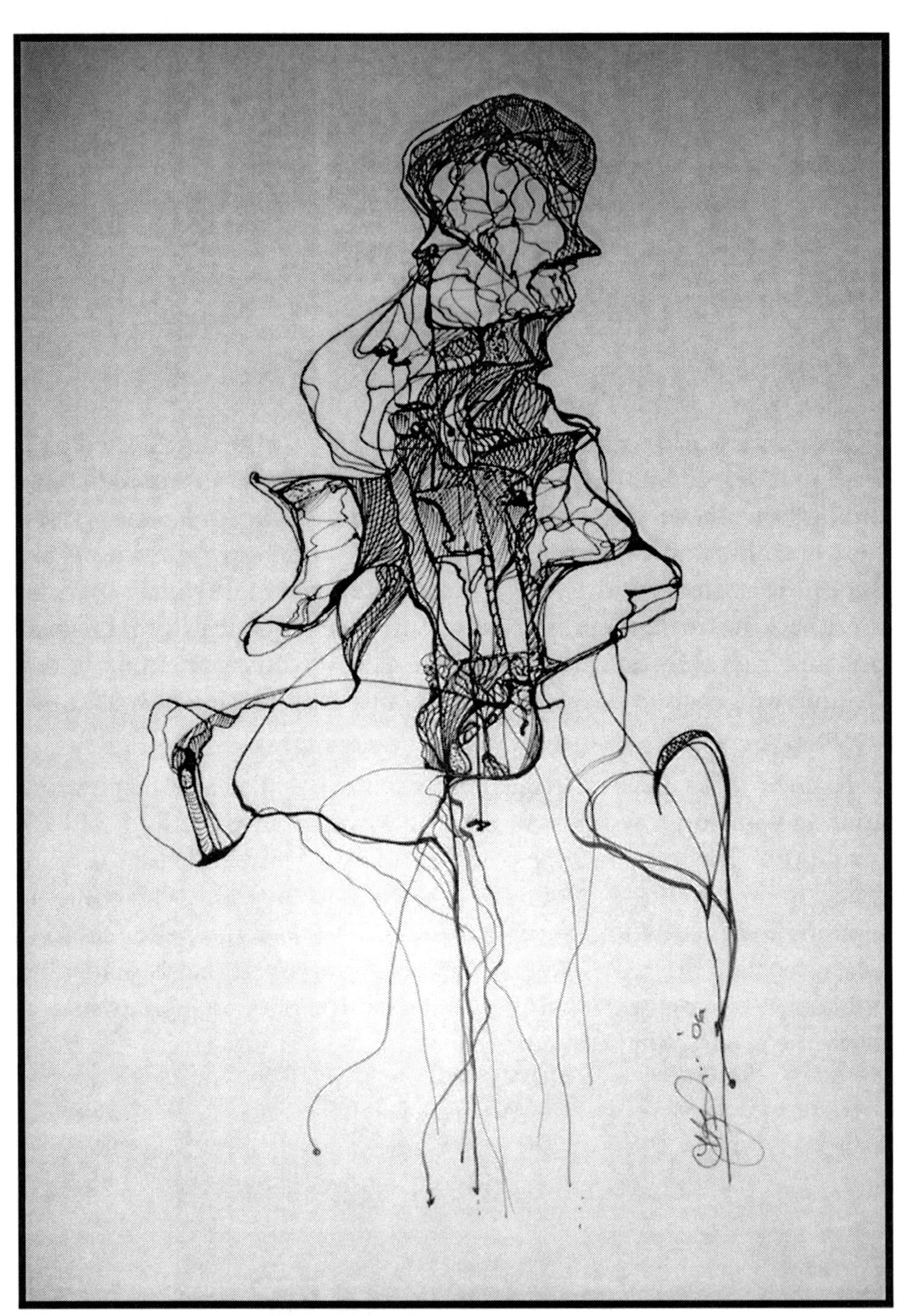

(Illustration created by Author.)

DEGREE TWO: ROOT

Imagine a world without suffering. Do you wake up every morning believing that you have a fortunate life? Learn how to create integrity as protection and sidestep negative energies, confrontations and less than favorable circumstances. Rely on your intuition and cultivate a new flexibility in your RADICAL ROOT mind. When the mind suffers it finds gratification in creating shields. Dig deep and hold the essence of your being, finding the rare and beautiful within.

There are many forms of abuse and sometimes we believe that circumstances will never change and our hope for peace of mind never realized, this is not true.

Inspired to be Rewired is a tenacious attempt to share real life experiences with empathy in the hope that at the base of your suffering there is a desire to empower yourself to change. Whether in business, partnerships or facing disease you can remove obstacles and eliminate the root of your suffering. Work through your RADICAL ROOT issues by following the five steps which include identifying, measuring, renaming, projecting and creating. There is an artist inside of everyone. Walk through the door of change.

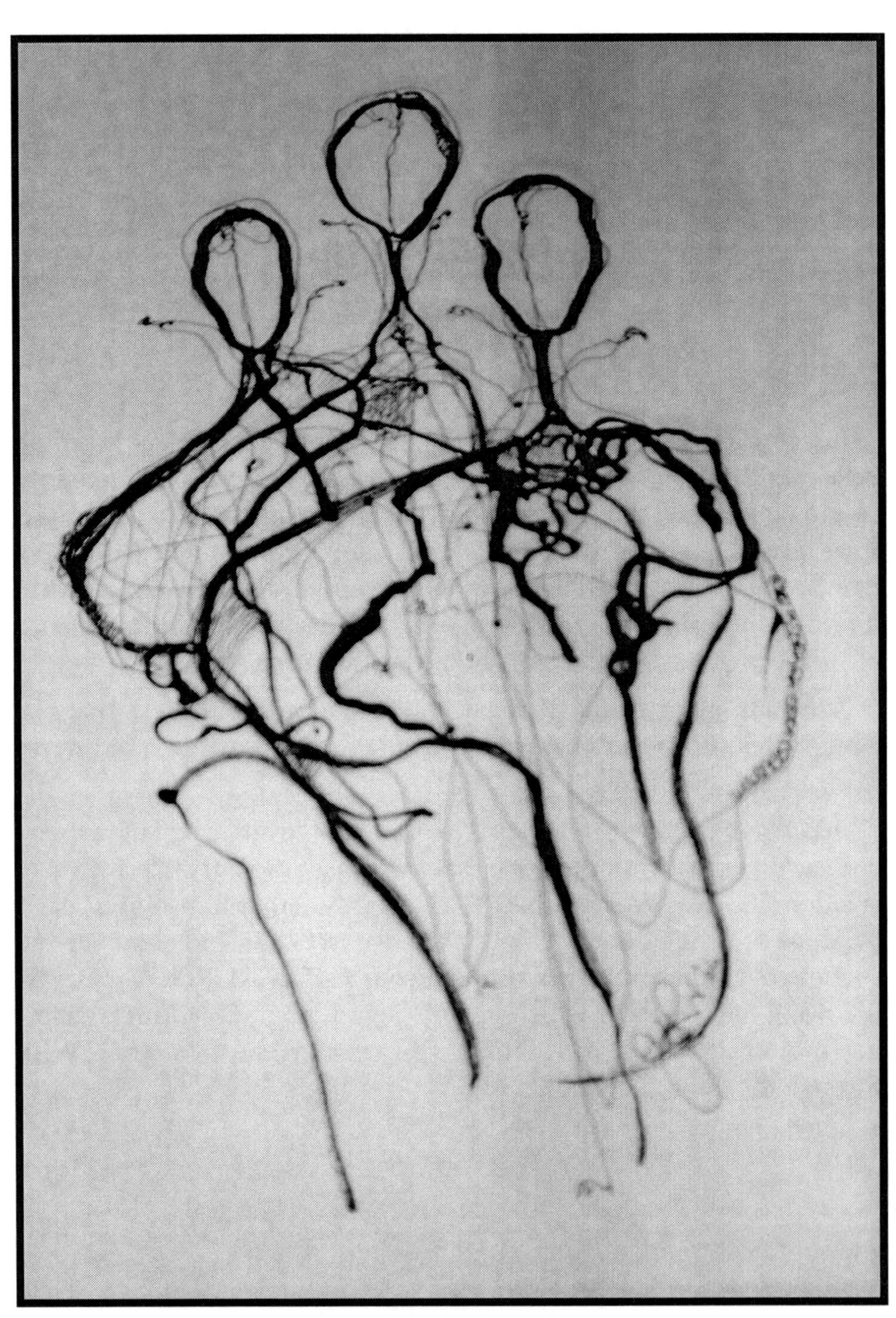

(Illustration created by Author.)

DEGREE THREE: REMEDY

Imagine a world that is finally at Peace and you are the harbinger of that moment. We actually have all the knowledge and rights of freedom to make this a reality. Is it not true that we do better in business when we do better by and for each other? Take inventory of your life based on the RADICAL REMEDY guidelines. Execute a commitment to action and become a steward of your integrity. The steps to healing are expedient and the courage and stamina that you will require are tools simply waiting for you to open. We are procrastinators. When we realize that facing issues with common sense and mindfulness will not only ease our own suffering but actually embrace the suffering of those we are in relationship with the healings begin.

The RADICAL REMEDY becomes a by-pass to happiness and healing. The value added is exponential. The inclination to be critical of ourselves dissolves. We erase the old pathway and create better outcomes. *Inspired to be Rewired* outlines the diversions and remedies that will nurture and strengthen the restoration of your attitude resulting in a better quality of life.

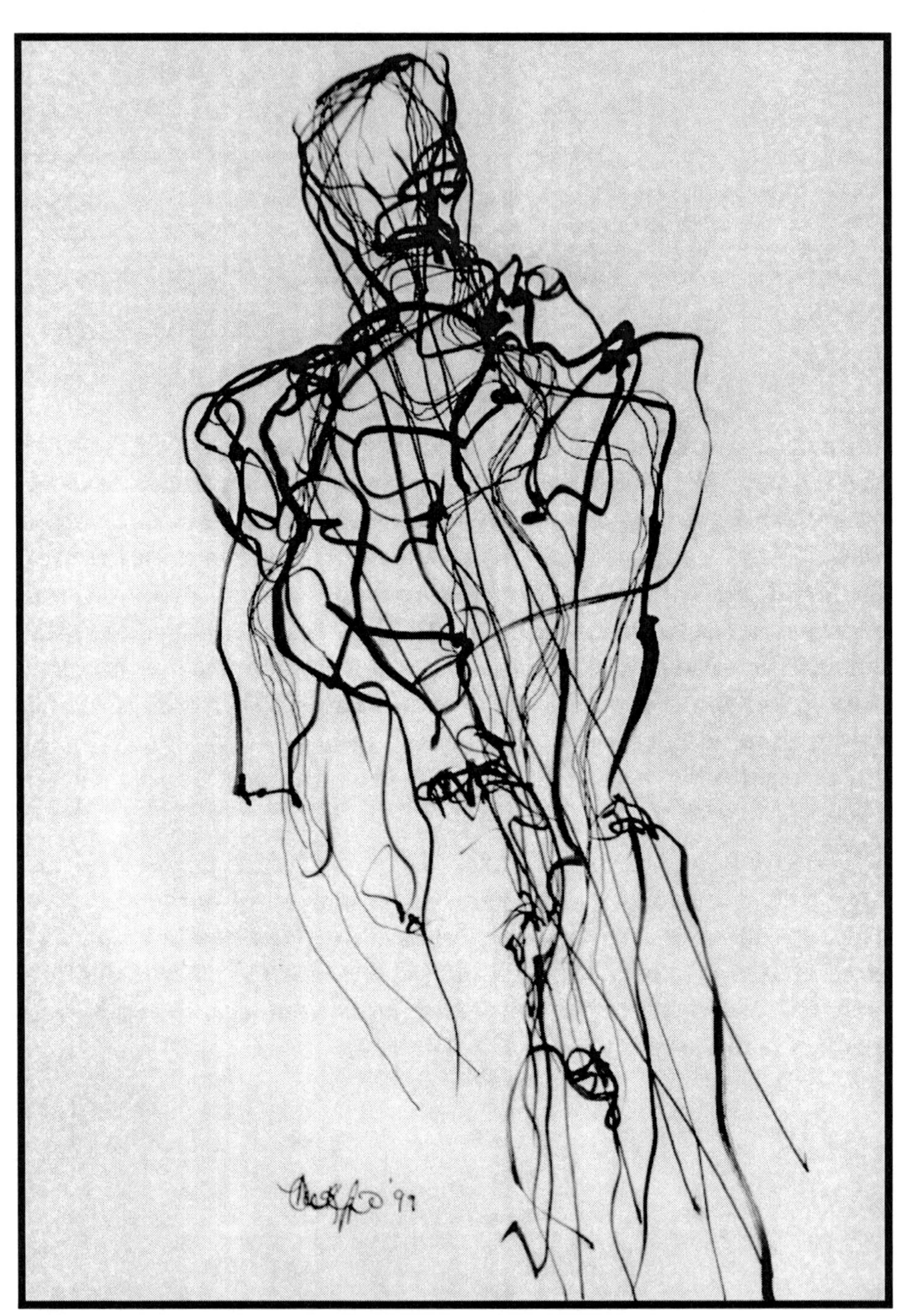

(Illustration created by Author.)

DEGREE FOUR: REALIZATION

Imagine that your life had transcended all your fears, problems and chaos. What if you actually woke up one day and believed in seeing the sanctity and beauty of life regardless of race, colour, creed or sex? What if you had transcended to become a prominent world citizen with a vision for the future that touched every nerve in every human audience? The RADICAL REALIZATION is that you are already achieving and creating your future by actively acknowledging that you want to be part of the Mystery of life. You hold the integrity and sheer fun of participating when you give yourself permission to raise your awareness, jump outside of your "usual" and penetrate a little deeper into the Attitude that you have manifested. With great self-confidence through awareness and mindfulness you will shift your life, business and outcomes. All that you yearn for is attainable.

We are all searching for meaning. There is a significant need in the workplace to unravel crisis after crisis as we cope with a pace of change that is at warp speed. RADICAL REALIZATION is achievable when you enter into the Mastering of the Five Degrees. Seek equanimity and operate with a mind free of delusions.

(Illustration created by Author.)

DEGREE FIVE: REALITY

Impermanence

Overcoming stage fright on your death bed

Forgiveness

Listen and understand with your heart open. There will always be challenges. We co-exist to experience our awareness through consciousness. When you develop a strong will to shift the focus from the vicissitudes of your own life to the well-being of others that is when the transformation happens. We begin living with true happiness, true compassion and true reverence for life. Create your own RADICAL REALITY thinking with the understanding that this is the time to see things as they really are. Do not run the RADICAL RISK of losing this rare opportunity to practice as a good world citizen. Your actions count now. Invite yourself to the table of eternity and prepare your mind for its feast. Live with integrity as your protector and an attitude that is re-humanized.

If just one person opens their radiant mind to receive what is attainable, pliable and workable then we together are creating a World of Peace.

DEFINITION OF TERMS

KARMA: Karma literally "action" is intentional and deliberate movement of the mind or consciousness. It is through this action our body, speech and mind become activated to do, say and think in a certain way. This activity creates karmic imprints or potencies that ripen through the unfolding of the individual's life. This law of cause and result is definite in that a wholesome imprint made by doing, saying, or thinking something positive results in happiness for the individual. Adversely, negative behaviors ripen in the suffering for the individual. One cannot experience the result of someone else's karma and the potency is never lost over time. Therefore, carrying out wholesome activities leads to benefit for oneself, and, the opposite will result in negative consequences.

(Venerable Amy Miller, www.milarepacenter.org)

ALIBI: The noun ALIBI is the same word as its Latin root, alibi, which means "excuse." When you provide an alibi, you are giving proof—a certified excuse.

MONKEY BLOOD: Nickname of Mercurochrome Antiseptic.

TIGER BLOOD: Nickname of Merthiolate (or Iodine).

WHAT IS YOUR KARMIC ALIBI?

In this book Patricia shared insight into her personal motivations, detailing how the hand of fate changed her life on a multitude of occasions, always driving her forward to succeed in new ways.

Please take a moment to answer the following questions:

1. Am I holding onto an event in my life that I cannot get over?
2. Am I suffering from this event?
3. Am I holding someone else accountable for that event whether I understood the circumstances or not?
4. Am I willing to change?

If you answered yes to the fourth question, you have made the first step in Mastering the Five Radical Degrees of life.

Please check the website of http://www.inspiredtoberewired.com for future exercises, information and a companion workbook.

Contact: http://www.inspiredtoberewired.com

Those who read this book and take the journey with me will achieve the Five Radical Degrees of life and will create new pathways to personal awareness. Integrity will be your protector and compassion the common expression of your being.

ABOUT THE AUTHOR: PATRICIA KAREN GAGIC

Patricia Gagic is an International Contemporary Artist, Photographer and Author. She was born in 1953 in Montreal, Quebec Canada to parents of European decent. Her career achievements include senior management in Banking, self-employed business owner in Property and Medical Management.

She is an Advisor to the Board of Free the Children, an Ambassador with Friends to Mankind and co-founded the Colors of Freedom Foundation. She supports many initiatives including the Ambassadors for World Peace and the Foundation for the Preservation of the Mahayana Tradition. She is dedicated to a school and orphanage in Angkor Wat, Cambodia. Patricia is a member of the Ontario Cabinet of Friends of the Canadian Museum for Human Rights.

Patricia is a Certified Applied Mindfulness Specialist in Meditation, certified by Mindfulness without Borders to facilitate Ambassador Council and continues her studies at the University of Toronto in Transformative Mindfulness. She is a Certified Feng Shui Level II Consultant and Reiki Master. Nominated and recipient of many Awards including Status of Women in Canada; appointment to the Board of Governors of Junior Achievement; YMCA Peace Medal; YWCA Woman of Distinction Lifetime Achievement; and first Award of Excellence from the Toronto Women's Expo. She is represented by Gallery on the Bay in Hamilton, Ontario and International Fine Arts in Caslano, Switzerland. Patricia was cast in the "Life Story Project" a documentary series by OWN (Oprah Winfrey Network). In 2013 Patricia was knighted as a Dame of the Order of St. George.

To contact: www.PatriciaGagic.com

ACKNOWLEDGMENTS

There are champions and heroes in my life, lovely friends and family who protect, love and make me feel special. There are some who become our teachers and challenge us to be better human beings. When my vision for this book was being mapped out there were many more insights and experiences I considered worthy of inclusion. What sifted out has become a glimpse into my heart, a dance through my mind and a sharing of how life has been full. The glass is not half empty it was poured and refilled many times by all who have touched my life.

As I hold the beacon of light in front of me, I shine it on all of you who have made a difference in my life. We can never underestimate the power or impact of any one person. It is a daunting task to retrieve all the names of those who have made measure in my life and I ask forgiveness if I accidently have not mentioned you. The evidence lies inside the quilt of my heart where I have stitched your names forever.

I am deeply grateful to Bettie Youngs of Bettie Youngs Book Publishers, who is a breath of fresh air, a ray of sunshine and true blessing! The dedication to your authors is outstanding. You are a beautiful treasure. Thank you so much for all of your support and to Jazmin Gomez for her lovely design and typesetting of this book.

Ned, I offer my deepest gratitude for your encouragement and support. I will never forget standing in front of the Coda Gallery in New York City as you said, "From your mouth to God's ears." This has been a constant reminder that all things are possible.

I am so blessed to have met and have the privilege of being mentored by the wonderful actor and motivational humanitarian Glenn Morshower. Glenn examines life with a grand spirit and your work is inspirational on and off camera. Glenn goes "the Extra Mile" and is a revolutionary soul. Thank you for reading my work and writing the foreword. I am deeply grateful.

I acknowledge my spiritual mentors. With gratefulness I bow low to all my teachers. Our Beloved Jeshua, Pope Francis, the late Pope John Paul, Bahaullah, His Holiness the 14th Dalai Lama, Lama Zopa Rinpoche, Thupten Rinpoche, the late Master Yu Tian Jian, Master Keo Ann, the late Adi Da Samraj, Dhyan Vimal, Thich Nhat Hahn, Dekyi Lee Oldershaw, Michele Chaban, Venerable Amy Miller, John of God, Dr.Budhendranauth Doobay, Monsignor Brad Massman, Theo Koffler, Dr. Joe Dispenza, Matthieu Ricard, Dr. Richard Davidson, Marcia Small, Glenn Mullin, Pema Chodron, Gail Bauer, Furtemba Sherpa, Deepak Chopra, Dr. Wayne Dyer, Stephen Izreal, Gordon Davidson and Corinne McLaughlin, the late David R. Hawkins and to my precious "Mothers" Helen, Gladys, Caroline, Olga and Radana.

My protector Palden Lhamo and the Black Maddona.

My best friend Kathy Jo Stark, a light in my life since Grade Three!

I am grateful for the kindness and support of my precious family, my mother Helen, Sister Debbie (Len), loving nieces Rebecca (Cam), Emily (Eddie) and nephew Christopher (Nicole) you drew me into your circle of love and made a difference in my life. I acknowledge the late Mike Skura. Not a day goes by without a smile remembering the unconditional love and incredible support from the late Jack Davidson.

I honor the Roberts family who will forever live in my heart and taught me so much about life and love… Daniel McGuire you are a special one, your parents the late Olga and Leslie, brothers Miles (Meeka) and Lindsay (Lori), sister Pat (Bob) and all their families.

To my library angel Miss Meeps who has sat on the computer, the desk, the chair, my lap, the papers and never once complained I was up too late! Kota you are the family protector.

I wish to thank my beautiful daughter Kyra for her constancy and incredible courage reminding me how only this moment matters. I am grateful for you as my perfect teacher. Charlie you have filled our lives with your genius. Cyris you are the most perfect angel who has experienced life beyond your years and will watch Matilda with Gaia forever!

Gabriel will follow in your footsteps. My love to the late Christopher Boss who was a priceless gem gone too soon.

Inspiration and love came from the beautiful hearts of the late Mile and Radana Gagic who instilled tolerance and forgiveness with a great passion for education. Alexandra, Jeff, Julia, Rachel, Christopher, Sandra, Dr. Predrag and Marina Gagic, Dr. Ksenija and Dr. Scott Belsley, Nena and Tanja Roglic and all the Calgary and Edmonton clan, you are each fondly held in my heart. A special thank you to Chris and Marvin Foster your love and friendship has spanned a quarter century and I have deep respect and love for you.

Judy Suke, you are my angel and beautiful friend… you offer flawless and endless support. Burning the candle after midnight on so many occasions and holding court with me through all the rough stages, deadlines and manuscript preparation. I am grateful for your time, expertise and brilliant ideas! I also love your ability to make me really laugh out loud.

Sharon Babineau, you are an endless source of wisdom, creativity and a cornucopia of brilliant ideas. While we met on the doorstep of sorrow we have overcome much, sharing smiles and laughter. Move over Thelma and Louise. Praise to your beautiful son Derek for his sincerity and kindness, the late Maddison for her gift of selflessness and Arunas for your spirit and friendship. You are all treasures in my life.

I wish to honor the late Jigme Norbu (founder of the Ambassadors for World Peace) his wife Yaling and children. Donna Kim Brand you care deeply about the world and have inspired many! Thank you for inviting me to attend Craig Duswalt's RockStar Marketing BootCamp. It not only turned my life inside out but put the gears in motion to write this book. Donna you are a guiding light. Craig Duswalt, you are the greatest source of encouragement anyone could ever hope or ask for. Your light shines not only from the stage but from heaven above. Thank you Natasha, your three wonderful children and parents Anne and Anton who are love and kindness personified.

I cherish and respect the creative genius and generous heart of the artist Dragan Dragic, his beautiful wife Sylvie and sons Jovan and Rajko. Without doubt you have had the most significant impact on my life. Dragan you are a very precious friend.

I acknowledge my fellow RockStars and Master Minds who have given me great ideas. Wisdom and creativity pour through the veins of each of you. I give a shout out to Furman Meggett, Trish Ellis, Karen Strauss, Maryann Ehmann, Hidi Lee, Maurice DiMino, Heather Hansen O'Neill, Bonnie Kitahata, Larry Broughton, Adam Ace, Helen Woo, Maurice Slaton, Barbara Allison, Randy and Susan Cooper, Kathy da Silva, Carol Shockley, Randy Gold, Christopher Rausch, Eric Tonningsen, Ricky Powell, Kristen Sharma, Carol Pilkington, Forest Fisher, Merv Jersak, Teresa Vilardi Bridget Brady and Ernie Hudson. We are a powerful resource to one another!

Serinda Swan and Alandra Napoli Kai both of you have influenced and graced my life. I cherish our friendships.

I honor the late Allan Silberhartz, Executive Director of Bridging Heaven and Earth and a very good friend.

Nima and Owen McElhinney, Dawa, L.G.Khambache and family together you hold a very precious place in my heart, gifting me with the "bead" of wisdom from Venerable Ani Ngawang Pema Sherpa. As evidence in the power of karma and change, I bow low. I also acknowledge the late Sir Edmund Hilary.

Master Keo ann, your spirit and efforts inspire me to work even harder. My life is blessed by the patience and commitment you offer to the monks and children at the Pagoda Thmey in Angkor Wat, Cambodia. I dedicate the merit of this book to all of you.

Craig and Mark Kielburger Co-founders of Free the Children have an understanding of equanimity in this world. You are both examples of selflessness and humility. You have opened up a plethora of new ideas to the world with integrity and faith. I acknowledge your incredible commitment to inspiring change. I am deeply proud to call you my friends.

So many have been have been part of my journey and will forever be in my heart. To each of you I wish I could write a special thank you but it would be another book!

I consider myself so lucky to have the love and friendship of my dearest friend Nadine Lucki who has a brilliant mind and keeps me thinking "out of the box." A soul sister!

To the Colours of Freedom Foundation members you have gifted me with love and inspiration. As I write the names of those who have touched my life, I also ask forgiveness if I have missed a few!

Linda Rosier, Joseph Catalano, the late Donna Penrice and Marcia Stanley, Terry Guest, HHR Duke of York, Liz Armstrong the late Sylvia Morawetz, Norma Gamble, Diane Cruz, Paddie Lucas, Janice Dolson, Kathy Doore, Lynda Henriksen, Ruth Dwyer, Catherine,Blair, Keltie and Kailee Baldwin, my wonderful friend Marlaise Dawson, my studio partners Dr. David Dawson and Barry Hodgson, Brent Moody, Jordan Moody, Somaly Mam, Barbara Brant, Gail Whitlow, Wayne Strongman, Dianna Dinevski, Jane McCormick, Jane George, Donna Lojek, Dr. Cindy Hamielec, Alipa Patel, Scott Henderson, Ray Harris, Brian Melo, Viga Boland, Victoria Boland, Andrew Rudd, Kristal Vanderkruk, Ludlow Bailey, Deborah and Ron Seigel, Cordula Ehms and Ray Wilkins, Leigh Blake, Karen Morrissey, Sheilagh Hagens, Geoff Burchell, Fred and Dora Bianchi, Patricia Ann Brooks, Amanda Owen, Elizabeth Skronski, Karen Wight, Roza Lukovic, Kim Callaghan, Gisele Theriault, Judy Papalia, Dianne Bekkedam, Blake Bliss, Una West, Dr. Jacqlyn Pogue, Alex and Susan Gilbert, Jim and Stephanie McLean, Fern Brown, David Lane, Jim Cimba, Sam Alaimo, Jarek Rodycz, Zack Pospieszynski, Jacki Harkness, Dr. Chande, George Seehaver and Marianne Lattanzi, Dr. Rose Jeans, Lori Goldblatt, the late Florence Sicoli, Pamela Jones, Isabelle Katz, Julia Guth, Alexander Green, Aharon Ipale, Andre Miripolsky, P.J. Mercanti, Justin Joseph, Aron Burch, Mark Tharme, Judy Boswell, Jill McDonald, Ana Montero, Darlene Ondi, Ryan Furlong, Ashley Cooper, Filip Cederholm, Debra Vivian, Dr. Nancy Zak, Susie Parazader, Matthew Varey, Anna Balla, Jan Ridge, Katie Keenleyside, Jacob Moon, Linda McDowell, Charles and Margaret Juravinski, Gulam, Dr. Mary Syty-Golda, Dave Gould, Hajni Yosifov, Teri McLuhan, Gerry Morelli, Michael and Trudy Jay, Leah Gardiner, Bev and Manny Blicker, Kathy and Michael Skerritt, Holly Corder, Jack Blum and Sharon Corder, Jackie Wilkinson, Winona girls Kathy, Debbie and Carol you rock! The book writing gals Gloria Christianson and Ruth Church.

Dr. Zen and Lena Kiss, Dr. Trevor Seaton, Kathryn and Sonny Palumbo, Randi Goodman, Madlen Satz, Irene Cara, Bob Lanois, Tom and Beverly Hogue, Bob Daniels, Tony Urquhart, Dr. Marko Simuno vic and Colina Maxwell, Charlie Anne Courchesne, Tomi Swick, Laura Swick, Joanne Greene, the late Conrad Furey, Wolf and Jana Bottinelli, Jacob Moon, Gary Roy, David Peck, Dr. Andrea Frolic, Anna Balla, Min Joo Lee, James Awad, Ana Montero, Prince Randy Alam-Sogan, Renee Hodgkinson, Amanda Lindhout, Precious Chong, Yoti, Fern and Tina Telio, Isabel, Diana, Marina, Anouchka and George Tintor, Laura Hollick. GLV friends, Sandy Peckinpah, The Boss family, Phyllis and Michael, Carreen and family, Jim De Girolamo, Carol Lorrayne, Sothany Peung, Phanith Bou, Adele, Alberta Butler, Jordan Bowman, Carol Wiggins, Dalal al-waheidi, Vilia Nekrasas, fellow Dames and Knights to the Order of St. George and all my TMM and AMM cohorts from the University of Toronto. Shelley Urlando, Bob Bryden, John, Joe and Dolores Sudak, The Cihocki, Shibish and Panchezak families, Stan and Marie Semeniuk and families, Led Zeppelin, Leonard Cohen, Deva Premal, Miten, Manish Vyas, Manose, Portishead, Radiohead, Glenn Gould, Jan Garbarek, Lana del Ray and U2. Thank you for the music!

I honor my late grandparents, Anthony, Gladys, Nicholas and Caroline.

To each and all of you, a heartfelt thank you.

(Testimonials continued from the front of this book …)

"*KARMIC ALIBI* is a life changing book! Patricia masters the technique of teaching us how to reconnect to our natural powerful selves. When we recognize our emptiness and desire to be REWIRED, Patricia Gagic is the teacher fulfilling her calling for us." **—Furman Meggett, Author, Speaker, Spoken Word Artist, Los Angeles, California (www.furmanmeggett.com)**

"*KARMIC ALIBI* is a truly extraordinary and sensitive book. Patricia has a way of getting to the profound heart of the matter (any matter) with an ocean of compassion, but also with simple, practical wisdom. She reveals this in *Karmic Alibi.* When you finish this book you will feel soothed and clear." **—Jack Blum (www.ReelCanada.com)**

"Few people hold the belief that they can change the world. Even fewer hold the brilliance to make it happen. I believe Patricia Karen Gagic is one of those few. Patricia represents loving compassion for humanity and a deep desire to inspire greater consciousness on this earth. In *Karmic Alibi* she offers us inspiration and teachings for a sustainable future and a means to world peace. Patricia is the shining light on the path to a new era for mankind." **—Trish Ellis, Speaker, Life Coach, Author, (www.insearchofbliss.com)**

"Patricia Gagic is one of those rare individuals where you can feel her beauty and wisdom from across the room … and as you get closer and talk with her this feeling of compassion and integrity only deepens." **—Heather Hanson O'Neill, President Find Your Fire in Five (www.fireinfive.com)**

"Patricia Gagic is a brilliant creative mind who has a passion to help others. I witnessed her strength of community goodwill worldwide. *Karmic Alibi* is written to show us we all have the ability to live with a loving heart and can make the future for others much better with mindfulness and compassion. This book is an encouragement to all and an inspiration for a better life. Patricia gives her time and spirit for no other reason than to make you feel inspired through challenging times." **—Alipa Patel**

"One of the most amazing things about ABC Charity is the way it brings together not only kids but adults alike from all over the world and encourages them to live from their hearts. When I met Patricia, there was an instant soul connection extending from a mutual desire to nurture love in this world. She is a true warrior of peace on this planet and *KARMIC ALIBI* reminds us again, how we are all part of a Global family." **—Ashley Cooper, Co-Founder *ABC Charity***

"When I started reading *KARMIC ALIBI*, I had no idea it would be a book I could not put down. From cover to cover every sentence was a message written in and out of time. The depth of emotion portrayed catches you off guard and demands your full attention. I loved this book and will tell everyone 'run don't walk' to get *KARMIC ALIBI* in your hands. This book is a keeper!" **—Anne Patchell Duswalt, Deer Park, New York**

"In *KARMIC ALIBI* Patricia shares her unusual destiny. This book made me weep and also marvel at Patricia's strength to handle and transform her challenges with formidable courage. In many cultures, the telling of your story and passing on its life lessons is an essential gift to preserve wisdom. Patricia has done this from the heart. I highly recommend *Karmic Alibi*."**—Nadine Lucki, 2020 Vision Leadership Initiatives**

Other Books by Bettie Youngs Book Publishers

Hostage of Paradox: A Qualmish Disclosure

John Rixey Moore

Few people then or now know about the clandestine war that the CIA ran in Vietnam, using the Green Berets for secret operations throughout Southeast Asia. This was not the Vietnam War of the newsreels, the body counts, rice paddy footage, and men smoking cigarettes on the sandbag bunkers. This was a shadow directive of deep-penetration interdiction, reconnaissance, and assassination missions conducted by a selected few Special Forces units, deployed quietly from forward operations bases to prowl through agendas that, for security reasons, were seldom understood by the men themselves.

Hostage of Paradox is the first-hand account by one of these elite team leaders.

"Deserving of a place in the upper ranks of Vietnam War memoirs." **—Kirkus Review**

"Read this book, you'll be, as John Moore puts it, 'transfixed, like kittens in a box.'" **—David Willson, Book Review, The VVA Veteran**

ISBN: 978-1-936332-37-3 • ePub: 978-1-936332-33-5

The Maybelline Story

And the Spirited Family Dynasty Behind It

Sharrie Williams

A fascinating and inspiring story, a tale both epic and intimate, alive with the clash, the hustle, the music, and dance of American enterprise.

"A richly told story of a forty-year, white-hot love triangle that fans the flames of a major worldwide conglomerate." **—Neil Shulman, Associate Producer, *Doc Hollywood***

"Salacious! Engrossing! There are certain stories so dramatic, so sordid, that they seem positively destined for film; this is one of them." ***—New York Post***

ISBN: 978-0-9843081-1-8 • ePub: 978-1-936332-17-5

Last Reader Standing
. . . The Story of a Man Who Learned to Read at 54

Archie Willard
with Colleen Wiemerslage

The day Archie lost his thirty-one year job as a laborer at a meat packing company, he was forced to confront the secret he had held so closely for most of his life: at the age of fifty-four, he couldn't read. For all his adult life, he'd been able to skirt around the issue. But now, forced to find a new job to support his family, he could no longer hide from the truth.

Last Reader Standing is the story of Archie's amazing—and often painful—journey of becoming literate at middle age, struggling with the newfound knowledge of his dyslexia. From the little boy who was banished to the back of the classroom because the teachers labeled him "stupid," Archie emerged to becoming a national figure who continues to enlighten professionals into the world of the learning disabled. He joined Barbara Bush on stage for her Literacy Foundation's fundraisers where she proudly introduced him as "the man who took advantage of a second chance and improved his life."

This is a touching and poignant story that gives us an eye-opening view of the lack of literacy in our society, and how important it is for all of us to have opportunity to become all that we can be—to have hope and go after our dreams.

At the age of eighty-two, Archie continues to work with literacy issues in medicine and consumerism.

> "Archie . . . you need to continue spreading the word." —**Barbara Bush, founder of the Literacy Foundation, and First Lady and wife of George H. W. Bush, the 41st President of the United States**

ISBN: 978-1-936332-48-9 • ePub: 978-1-936332-50-2

Fastest Man in the World
The Tony Volpentest Story

Tony Volpentest
Foreword by Ross Perot

Tony Volpentest, a four-time Paralympic gold medalist and five-time world champion sprinter, is a 2012 nominee for the Olympic Hall of Fame. This inspirational story details his being born without feet, to holding records as the fastest sprinter in the world.

> "This inspiring story is about the thrill of victory to be sure—winning gold—but it is also a reminder about human potential: the willingness to push ourselves beyond the ledge of our own imagination. A powerfully inspirational story." —**Charlie Huebner, United States Olympic Committee**

ISBN: 978-1-940784-07-6 • ePub: 978-1-940784-08-3

Company of Stone

John Rixey Moore

With yet unhealed wounds from recent combat, John Moore undertook an unexpected walking tour in the rugged Scottish highlands. With the approach of a season of freezing rainstorms he took shelter in a remote monastery—a chance encounter that would change his future, his beliefs about blind chance, and the unexpected courses by which the best in human nature can smuggle its way into the life of a stranger. Afterwards, a chance conversation overheard in a village pub steered him to Canada, where he took a job as a rock drill operator in a large industrial gold mine. The dangers he encountered among the lost men in that dangerous other world, secretive men who sought permanent anonymity in the perils of work deep underground—a brutal kind of monasticism itself—challenged both his endurance and his sense of humanity.

With sensitivity and delightful good humor, Moore explores the surprising lessons learned in these strangely rich fraternities of forgotten men—a brotherhood housed in crumbling medieval masonry, and one shared in the unforgiving depths of the gold mine.

ISBN: 978-1-936332-44-1 • ePub: 978-1-936332-45-8

On Toby's Terms

Charmaine Hammond

On Toby's Terms is an endearing story of a beguiling creature who teaches his owners that, despite their trying to teach him how to be the dog they want, he is the one to lay out the terms of being the dog he needs to be. This insight would change their lives forever.

"This is a captivating, heartwarming story and we are very excited about bringing it to film." **—Steve Hudis, Producer**

ISBN: 978-0-9843081-4-9 • ePub: 978-1-936332-15-1

Blackbird Singing in the Dead of Night
What to Do When God Won't Answer

Updated Edition with Study Guide

Gregory L. Hunt

Pastor Greg Hunt had devoted nearly thirty years to congregational ministry, helping people experience God and find their way in life. Then came his own crisis of faith and calling. While turning to God for guidance, he finds nothing. Neither his education nor his religious involvements could prepare him for the disorienting impact of the experience. Alarmed, he tries an experiment. The result is startling—and changes his life entirely.

"Compelling. If you have ever longed to hear God whispering a love song into your life, read this book." **—Gary Chapman, *NY Times* bestselling author, *The Love Languages of God***

ISBN: 978-0-9882848-9-0 • ePub: 978-1-936332-52-6

The Rebirth of Suzzan Blac

Suzzan Blac

A horrific upbringing and then abduction into the sex slave industry would all but kill Suzzan's spirit to live. But a happy marriage and two children brought love—and forty-two stunning paintings, art so raw that it initially frightened even the artist. "I hid the pieces for 15 years," says Suzzan, "but just as with the secrets in this book, I am slowing sneaking them out, one by one by one." Now a renowned artist, her work is exhibited world-wide. A story of inspiration, truth and victory.

"A solid memoir about a life reconstructed. Chilling, thrilling, and thought provoking." **—Pearry Teo, Producer, *The Gene Generation***

ISBN: 978-1-936332-22-9 • ePub: 978-1-936332-23-6

Voodoo in My Blood

A Healer's Journey from Surgeon to Shaman

Carolle Jean-Murat, M.D.

Born and raised in Haiti to a family of healers, US trained physician Carolle Jean-Murat came to be regarded as a world-class surgeon. But her success harbored a secret: in the operating room, she could quickly intuit the root cause of her patient's illness, often times knowing she could help the patient without surgery. Carolle knew that to fellow surgeons, her intuition was best left unmentioned. But when the devastating earthquake hit Haiti and Carolle returned to help, she had to acknowledge the shaman she had become.

"This fascinating memoir sheds light on the importance of asking yourself, 'Have I created for myself the life I've meant to live?'" **—Christiane Northrup, M.D., author of the New York Times bestsellers: *Women's Bodies, Women's Wisdom***

ISBN: 978-1-936332-05-2 • ePub: 978-1-936332-04-5

Electric Living

The Science behind the Law of Attraction

Kolie Crutcher

An electrical engineer by training, Crutcher applies his in-depth knowledge of electrical engineering principles and practical engineering experience detailing the scientific explanation of why human beings become what they think. A practical, step-by-step guide to help you harness your thoughts and emotions so that the Law of Attraction will benefit you.

ISBN: 978-1-936332-58-8 • ePub: 978-1-936332-59-5

DON CARINA: *WWII Mafia Heroine*

Ron Russell

A father's death in Southern Italy in the 1930s—a place where women who can read are considered unfit for marriage—thrusts seventeen-year-old Carina into servitude as a "black widow," a legal head of the household who cares for her twelve siblings. A scandal forces her into a marriage to Russo, the "Prince of Naples." By cunning force, Carina seizes control of Russo's organization and disguising herself as a man, controls the most powerful of Mafia groups for nearly a decade.

"A woman as the head of the Mafia who shows her family her resourcefulness, strength and survival techniques. Unique, creative and powerful! This exciting book blends history, intrigue and power into one delicious epic adventure that you will not want to put down!" **—Linda Gray, Actress, *Dallas***

ISBN: 978-0-9843081-9-4 • ePub: 978-1-936332-49-6

Amazing Adventures of a Nobody

Leon Logothetis

From the Hit Television Series Aired in 100 Countries!

Tired of his disconnected life and uninspiring job, Leon Logothetis leaves it all behind—job, money, home, even his cell phone—and hits the road with nothing but the clothes on his back and five dollars in his pocket, relying on the kindness of strangers and the serendipity of the open road for his daily keep. Masterful story-telling!

"A gem of a book; endearing, engaging and inspiring." **—Catharine Hamm, Los Angeles Times Travel Editor**

ISBN: 978-0-9843081-3-2 • ePub: 978-1-936332-51-9

MR. JOE
Tales from a Haunted Life

Joseph Barnett and Jane Congdon

Do you believe in ghosts? Joseph Barnett didn't, until the winter he was fired from his career job and became a school custodian. Assigned the graveyard shift, Joe was confronted with a series of bizarre and terrifying occurrences.

"Thrilling, thoughtful, elegantly told. So much more than a ghost story." **—Cyrus Webb, CEO, Conversation Book Club**

ISBN: 978-1-936332-78-6 • ePub: 978-1-936332-79-3

Out of the Transylvania Night

Aura Imbarus
A Pulitzer-Prize entry

"I'd grown up in the land of Transylvania, homeland to Dracula, Vlad the Impaler, and worse, dictator Nicolae Ceausescu," writes the author. "Under his rule, like vampires, we came to life after sundown, hiding our heirloom jewels and documents deep in the earth." Fleeing to the US to rebuild her life, she discovers a startling truth about straddling two cultures and striking a balance between one's dreams and the sacrifices that allow a sense of "home."

"Aura's courage shows the degree to which we are all willing to live lives centered on freedom, hope, and an authentic sense of self. Truly a love story!" **—Nadia Comaneci, Olympic Champion**

ISBN: 978-0-9843081-2-5 • ePub: 978-1-936332-20-5

Living with Multiple Personalities
The Christine Ducommun Story

Christine Ducommun

Christine Ducommun was a happily married wife and mother of two, when—after moving back into her childhood home—she began to experience panic attacks and bizarre flashbacks. Eventually diagnosed with Dissociative Identity Disorder (DID), Christine's story details an extraordinary twelve-year ordeal unraveling the buried trauma of her forgotten past.

"Reminiscent of the Academy Award-winning *A Beautiful Mind,* this true story will have you on the edge of your seat. Spellbinding!" **—Josh Miller, Producer**

ISBN: 978-0-9843081-5-6 • ePub: 978-1-936332-06-9

The Tortoise Shell Code

V Frank Asaro

Off the coast of Southern California, the Sea Diva, a tuna boat, sinks. Members of the crew are missing and what happened remains a mystery. Anthony Darren, a renowned and wealthy lawyer at the top of his game, knows the boat's owner and soon becomes involved in the case. As the case goes to trial, a missing crew member is believed to be at fault, but new evidence comes to light and the finger of guilt points in a completely unanticipated direction. An action-packed thriller.

ISBN: 978-1-936332-60-1 • ePub: 978-1-936332-61-8

The Search for the Lost Army
The National Geographic and Harvard University Expedition

Gary S. Chafetz

In one of history's greatest ancient disasters, a Persian army of 50,000 soldiers was suffocated by a hurricane-force sandstorm in 525 BC in Egypt's Western Desert. No trace of this conquering army, hauling huge quantities of looted gold and silver, has ever surfaced.

Gary Chafetz, referred to as "one of the ten best journalists of the past twenty-five years," is a former Boston Globe correspondent and was twice nominated for a Pulitzer Prize by the Globe.

ISBN: 978-1-936332-98-4 • ePub: 978-1-936332-99-1

A World Torn Asunder
The Life and Triumph of Constantin C. Giurescu

Marina Giurescu, M.D.

Constantin C. Giurescu was Romania's leading historian and author. His granddaughter's fascinating story of this remarkable man and his family follows their struggles in war-torn Romania from 1900 to the fall of the Soviet Union. An "enlightened" society is dismantled with the 1946 Communist takeover of Romania, and Constantin is confined to the notorious Sighet penitentiary. Drawing on her grandfather's prison diary (which was put in a glass jar, buried in a yard, then smuggled out of the country by Dr. Paul E. Michelson—who does the FOREWORD for this book), private letters and her own research, Dr. Giurescu writes of the legacy from the turn of the century to the fall of Communism.

We see the rise of modern Romania, the misery of World War I, the blossoming of its culture between the wars, and then the sellout of Eastern Europe to Russia after World War II. In this sweeping account, we see not only its effects socially and culturally, but the triumph in its wake: a man and his people who reclaim better lives for themselves, and in the process, teach us a lesson in endurance, patience, and will—not only to survive, but to thrive.

"The inspirational story of a quiet man and his silent defiance in the face of tyranny."
—Dr. Connie Mariano, author of *The White House Doctor*

ISBN: 978-1-936332-76-2 • ePub: 978-1-936332-77-9

Diary of a Beverly Hills Matchmaker

Marla Martenson

Quick-witted Marla takes her readers for a hilarious romp through her days as an LA matchmaker where looks are everything and money talks. The Cupid of Beverly Hills has introduced countless couples who lived happily ever-after, but for every success story there are hysterically funny dating disasters with high-maintenance, out of touch clients. Marla writes with charm and self-effacement about the universal struggle to love and be loved.

ISBN 978-0-9843081-0-1 • ePub: 978-1-936332-03-8

The Morphine Dream

Don Brown with *Pulitzer nominated Gary S. Chafetz*

At 36, high-school dropout and a failed semi-professional ballplayer Donald Brown hit bottom when an industrial accident left him immobilized. But Brown had a dream while on a morphine drip after surgery: he imagined himself graduating from Harvard Law School (he was a classmate of Barack Obama) and walking across America. Brown realizes both seemingly unreachable goals, and achieves national recognition as a legal crusader for minority homeowners. An intriguing tale of his long walk—both physical and metaphorical. A story of perseverance and second chances. Sheer inspiration for those wishing to reboot their lives.

"An incredibly inspirational memoir." **—Alan M. Dershowitz, professor, Harvard Law School**

ISBN: 978-1-936332-25-0 • ePub: 978-1-936332-39-7

The Girl Who Gave Her Wish Away

Sharon Babineau
Foreword by Craig Kielburger

The Children's Wish Foundation approached lovely thirteen-year-old Maddison Babineau just after she received her cancer diagnosis. "You can have anything," they told her, "a Disney cruise? The chance to meet your favorite movie star? A five thousand dollar shopping spree?"

Maddie knew exactly what she wanted. She had recently been moved to tears after watching a television program about the plight of orphaned children. Maddie's wish? To ease the suffering of these children half-way across the world. Despite the ravishing cancer, she became an indefatigable fundraiser for "her children." In The Girl Who Gave Wish Away, her mother reveals Maddie's remarkable journey of providing hope and future to the village children who had filled her heart.

A special story, heartwarming and reassuring.

ISBN: 978-1-936332-96-0 • ePub: 978-1-936332-97-7

It Started with Dracula
The Count, My Mother, and Me

Jane Congdon

The terrifying legend of Count Dracula silently skulking through the Transylvania night may have terrified generations of filmgoers, but the tall, elegant vampire captivated and electrified a young Jane Congdon, igniting a dream to one day see his mysterious land of ancient castles and misty hollows. Four decades later she finally takes her long-awaited trip—never dreaming that it would unearth decades-buried memories, and trigger a life-changing inner journey. A memoir full of surprises, Jane's story is one of hope, love—and second chances.

ISBN: 978-1-936332-10-6 • ePub: 978-1-936332-11-3

The Aspiring Actor's Handbook

Molly Cheek and Debbie Zip

Concise and straightforward, The Aspiring Actor's Handbook is written for curious and aspiring actors to help them make informed decisions while pursuing this exciting career.

Veteran actresses Molly Cheek and Debbie Zipp have culled the wit and wisdom of a wide array of successful actors, from Beth Grant to Dee Wallace, and collected the kind of mentoring perspective so many in the business wish they'd had when they were just starting out. Get insider information and real-life experiences and personal stories that range from how to get your foot in the door to becoming a career actor. Get the inside scoop from successful veteran actors on how to work with agents and unions; manage finances; prepare for auditions; cope with rejection—and success—and much more.

ISBN: 978-1-940784-12-0 • ePub: 978-1-940784-02-1

The Predatory Lies of Anorexia
A Survivor's Story

Abby D. Kelly

"I want...I want you to think I am the smartest, the thinnest, the most beautiful..."

With these words, Abby Kelly encapsulates the overwhelming struggle of her 15-year bout with anorexia. Abby lays bare the reality of anorexia, beginning in her teenage years, when the predatory lies of the disease took root in her psyche as she felt pressured from family and peers for not being "enough." In her quest for a greater sense of personal power, she concludes "I'll be 'more', but it will be on my terms."

Her reasoning is a classic example as to why and how eating disorders dig in and persist as long as they do.

From this new self-awareness, Abby targets her body as the agent to show others that she is disciplined and focused. She sets out to restrict her food intake and adheres to an extreme schedule of exercise. While others close to Abby see a person who is dangerously thin, Abby, in fact, derives a sense of personal achievement from her weight loss.

Abby exposes the battles, defeats, and ultimate triumph—taking the reader on a poignant odyssey from onset to recovery, including how she set out to fool the many who tried to help her, from dietitians to therapists, from one inpatient treatment center after another, and reveals not only the victim's suffering, but that of those who love her.

This raw and passionate story eloquently describes how Abby finally freed herself from this life-threatening condition, and how others can find courage and hope for recovery, too.

"This beautifully written book paints an exacting picture of Anorexia, one that is sure to help legions of those suffering from this most serious and life-threatening condition."
—Amy Dardis, founder and editor of Haven Journal

ISBN: 978-1-940784-17-5 • ePub: 978-1-940784-18-2

Truth Never Dies

William C. Chasey

A lobbyist for some 40 years, William C. Chasey represented some of the world's most prestigious business clients and twenty-three foreign governments before the US Congress. His integrity never questioned. All that changed when Chasey was hired to forge communications between Libya and the US Congress. A trip he took with a US Congressman for discussions with then Libyan leader Muammar Qadhafi forever changed Chasey's life. Upon his return, his bank accounts were frozen, clients and friends had been advised not to take his calls.

Things got worse: the CIA, FBI, IRS, and the Federal Judiciary attempted to coerce him into using his unique Libyan access to participate in a CIA-sponsored assassination plot of the two Libyans indicted for the bombing of Pan Am flight 103. Chasey's refusal to cooperate resulted in a six-year FBI investigation and sting operation, financial ruin, criminal charges, and incarceration in federal prison.

> "A chilling narrative about the abuses of state power. Intriguing! Compelling. Important."
> **—Michael Reagan, Radio Host, Author, Commentator and Political Strategist**

> "An unprecedented first hand look into the chilling world of Libyan Leader Muammar Qadhafi by the man who risked it all to resolve the dispute between the United States and Libya over the Lockerbie bombing. This is sure to be an unforgettable motion picture."
> **—Peter Tomaszewicz, Producer, Truth Never Dies**

ISBN: 978-1-936332-46-5 • ePub: 978-1-936332-47-2

News Girls Don't Cry

Melissa McCarty

Today the host of ORA TV's Newsbreaker, and now calling Larry King her boss, Melissa McCarty worked her way up through the trenches of live television news. But she was also running away from her past, one of growing up in the roughest of neighborhoods, watching so many she knew—including her brother—succumb to drugs, gangs, and violence. It was a past that forced her to be tough and streetwise, traits that in her career as a popular television newscaster, would end up working against her.

Every tragic story she covered was a grim reminder of where she'd been. But the practiced and restrained emotion given to the camera became her protective armor even in her private life where she was unable to let her guard down—a demeanor that damaged both her personal and professional relationships. In News Girls Don't Cry, McCarty confronts the memory-demons of her past, exploring how they hardened her—and how she turned it all around.

An inspiring story of overcoming adversity, welcoming second chances, and becoming happy and authentic.

> "A battle between personal success and private anguish, a captivating brave tale of a woman's drive to succed and her tireless struggle to keep her family intact. The reader is pulled into Melissa's story… an honest account of the common battle of addiction." **—Susan Hendricks, CNN Headline News Anchor**

ISBN: 978-1-936332-69-4 • ePub: 978-1-936332-70-0

Cinderella and the Carpetbagger

Grace Robbins

Harold Robbins's steamy books were once more widely read than the Bible. His novels sold more than 750 million copies and created the sex-power-glamour genre of popular literature that would go on to influence authors from Jackie Collins and Jacqueline Susann to TV shows like Dallas and Dynasty. What readers don't know is that Robbins—whom the media had dubbed the "prince of sex and scandal"—actually "researched" the free-wheeling escapades depicted in his books himself . . . along with his drop-dead, gorgeous wife, Grace. Now, in this revealing tell-all, for the first time ever, Grace Robbins rips the covers off the real life of the international best-selling author.

The 1960s and '70s were decades like no others—radical, experimental, libertine. Grace Robbins chronicles the rollicking good times, peppering her memoir with anecdotes of her encounters with luminaries from the world of entertainment and the arts—not to mention most of Hollywood. The couple was at the center of a globetrotting jet set, with mansions in Beverly Hills, villas and yachts on the French Riviera and Acapulco. Their life rivaled—and often surpassed—that of the characters in his books. Champagne flowed, cocaine was abundant, and sex in the pre-AIDS era was embraced with abandon. Along the way, the couple agreed to a "modern marriage," that Harold insisted upon. With charm, introspection, and humor, Grace lays open her fascinating, provocative roller-coaster ride of a life—her own true Cinderella tale.

"This sweet little memoir's getting a movie deal." **—New York Post**

"I gulped down every juicy minute of this funny, outrageous memoir. You will not be able to put it down until the sun comes up." **—Rex Reed**

"Grace Robbins has written an explosive tell-all. Sexy fun." **—Jackie Collins**

"You have been warned. This book is VERY HOT!" **—Robin Leach, Lifestyles of the Rich & Famous**

ISBN: 978-0-9882848-2-1 • ePub: 978-0-9882848-4-5

Trafficking the Good Life

Jennifer Myers

Jennifer Myers had worked hard toward a successful career as a dancer in Chicago. But just as her star was rising, she fell for the kingpin of a drug trafficking operation. Drawn to his life of excitement, she soon acquiesced to driving marijuana across the country, making easy money she stacked in shoeboxes and spent like an heiress. Only time in a federal prison made her face up to and understand her choices. It was there, at rock bottom, that she discovered that her real prison was the one she had unwittingly made inside herself and where she could start rebuilding a life of purpose and ethical pursuit.

"In her gripping memoir Jennifer Myers offers a startling account of how the pursuit of an elusive American Dream can lead us to the depths of the American criminal underbelly. Her book is as much about being human in a hyper-materialistic society as it is about drug culture. When the DEA finally knocks on Myers' door, she and the reader both see the moment for what it truly is—not so much an arrest as a rescue." **—Tony D'Souza, author of Whiteman and Mule**

ISBN: 978-1-936332-67-0 • ePub: 978-1-936332-68-7

Bettie Youngs Books

We specialize in MEMOIRS
...books that celebrate
fascinating people
and remarkable

CPSIA information can be obtained at www.ICGtesting.com
Printed in the USA
LVOW12s1326130714

393975LV00001B/39/P

9 781940 784298